A Deep Gladness

Stories from the lives of
Ken and Lorraine Enright

as told to Gina Riendeau

First published by Dog Ear Publishing
4010 W. 86th Street, Ste H
Indianapolis, IN 46268
www.dogearpublishing.net

ISBN: 978-1-4575-2062-4

This book is printed on acid-free paper.

Printed in the United States of America

"The place where God calls you is the place where your deep gladness and the world's deep hunger meet."

—Frederick Buechner

Dedication

Dedicated to the memory of Ken Enright (1922–2006), whose life and partnership with Lorraine led each to know the gladness of God's sure calling.

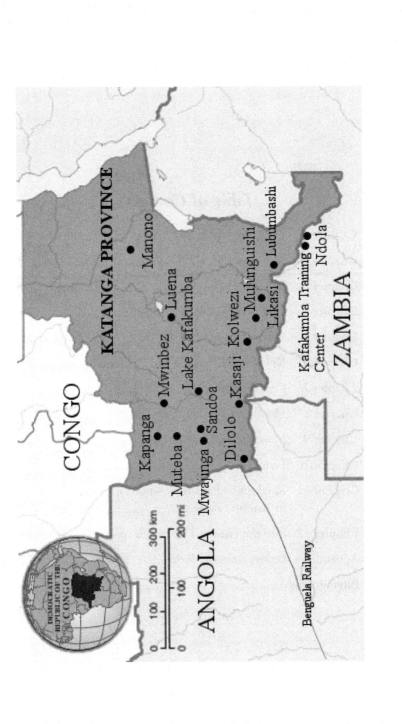

Table of Contents

From the author

It was obvious to me that neither Ken nor Lorraine Enright ever intended to have their stories told. They wrote no diaries, kept no journals, and no one had saved more than a handful of the letters they wrote to supporters over 60-plus years. Few pictures and almost no personal effects survived the multiple times their homes were ransacked by Congolese rebels. Both had resisted any suggestions to write a book, or any memoir, of their years in central Africa. In 2006 at the age of 84, Ken died of natural causes, right in the middle of that year's session of his beloved Pastors' School. He was buried at the Kafakumba Training Center in Zambia. With his death, the chance to tell their story seemed highly unlikely. And yet, in late 2011, at the age of 87, Lorraine Enright agreed with a friend's suggestion to share some of her memories as a missionary in Congo. The timing was right: Kafakumba Pastors' School would celebrate its 50-year anniversary in 2013, and an endowment had been established to provide a permanent source of funds for the school's operation. Lorraine wanted to support the endowment (named the Kafakumba Pastors' School Fund) by providing a brief history of the School's beginnings and of the role she and Ken played in its founding.

In February of 2012, I found myself in Lorraine's living room in Florida with a tape recorder and a cup of tea in hand. This book is the result of spending five days with Lorraine that February. She talked about Kafakumba Pastors' School and much more: about the families from which she and Ken came; about their years together in the field, complete with memories from each of their mission assignments; about highlights of their ministry, including Ken's love of flying and the founding of the aviation ministry, Wings of the Morning; about the founding of Kafakumba Pastors' School; about the years devoted to preaching, building churches, and developing leaders among churches and communities in Congo; about Lorraine's role in ministries of mercy—health, education, and a special love for working with young women and children; about their miraculous recovery from injuries suffered in several airplane crashes; about their release after being held captive by rebel soldiers in the 1978 Kolwezi Massacre; and about the sureness of their call to Congo and their lifelong certainty of being just where God wanted them to be.

In short, Lorraine agreed to this tiny glimpse into the life she and Ken shared for one reason: to recognize God's presence with them at all times, in all places. She was always mindful that they never worked alone and found it difficult to focus attention on herself or Ken. She recognized those who had come before, as well as the contributions of the missionaries and Congolese who were their contemporaries and who became like family. More than once, she commented that she wished we could "write a book about everybody." This humility was probably her greatest obstacle to writing a memoir. And by necessity, this writing is only the briefest of snapshots.

It remains impossible to capture the true depth and breadth of Ken and Lorraine's lives and work. It would have been a different story if Ken had told it. It would have been different if one of the Enright children told it (although I did spend some time with each of the adult Enright children, and some of their comments are included here), or different still if told in another time and place. But this is Lorraine's story. This is what she told me during those five days in February.

Several people helped me sort out some of the stories' details, and I thank them: John Enright, who provided insight into the ongoing development of the Pastors' School and details about their family's horrific captivity at the hands of rebels in

Kolwezi; fellow missionary, Lena Eschtruth, who filled in the medical details following Ken and Lorraine's last airplane crash; and son Ken Enright, who reviewed each chapter and wrote the foreword, reminding us that his parents' work was always a partnership with strong Congolese leadership and strengthened by a family of fellow missionaries and supporters. Thanks to Dru Smith for reading the manuscript and to the Enright and Huntzinger families for photos. Warren and Nancy Huntzinger harbored a dream to capture some stories from the lives of Ken and Lorraine Enright; their encouragement was invaluable.

Most of all, I thank Lorraine Enright for being open to a stranger—I grew to love her and her stories and her habit of drinking tea to celebrate the day's blessings. In the five days we spent together, I recognized a woman of immense courage, humility, and faith. She knew she had been where God wanted her to be. Even more, she remains assured of God's presence with her today, confident that she continues to be exactly where He wants her to be.

—Gina Riendeau

Note: The country called Congo in this book is the former Belgian Congo, known for years as Zaire, and today as the Democratic Republic of Congo. The Enright family refers to it simply as Congo.

All royalties and profits from the sale of this book benefit the Kafakumba Pastors' School to help train village pastors in Central Africa.

Foreword

This is a story centered in the middle of Africa, in villages far from the modern world. It is the story of Kenneth and Lorraine Enright, who were called to be missionaries in the Methodist Church in the Congo. It is the story of their friends, colleagues, and the ordinary people with whom they lived and worked to build God's Church in Africa and present the Good News of salvation.

They arrived in the Congo in 1950, in the middle of the 20th century. Some of the older people they first met were alive in the pre-colonial era, before the first white men arrived in central Africa. These men had seen tribal wars, famines, and slavery. Later, younger colleagues arose from the era of Congolese independence and were swept up in the subsequent fighting and chaos. All who worked with the Enrights during these years—doing God's work in Congo—experienced hardship, war, and illness. Some died of sickness. Some were killed in wars. All remained faithful and persistent and, in the end, victorious.

The church in Congo did not fall apart. The center has held. The church in southern Congo, in Katanga Province, has increased exponentially. The two Katanga United Methodist Conferences now include more than 8,000 congregations with membership approaching two million members. This story is not only about those who laid the foundation of the church in Congo and their adventures, but it is also about the hopes for their successors and the future. And, one of the critical means to ensure successors emerge is to continue the work of the Kafakumba Pastors' School, which today is training those who will continue God's work in the villages and towns of Central Africa in the future.

I am Kenneth Nelson Enright, Ken and Lorraine's eldest son. (I am referred to in the book as Kenny.) As I read Gina's account of my mother's stories, my memory comes alive with images of the people and places with which I grew up. There is Pastor Silas Mwamba's smiling face and laughter around a campfire. I can see the blacksmith, Rafael, showing me how to hammer hot iron into hoes with a hand-operated forge. I remember Muteba, a tough, powerful, old-guard Lunda chief carefully explaining to me that he was not donating the burnt bricks and construction materials to the Methodists to build two elementary schools in his area out of any personal or public virtue. He was doing it to force my father—his best friend—to visit him more often, as my father would now need to personally oversee construction of the schools. He ended his explanation with a very satisfied smile. I remember the wonderful smell of the wood smoke from the cooking fires at dusk in the villages where we stayed, the kindness of their welcomes, their gifts of chickens and eggs. Then there are the pictures in my mind of my mother talking with the village women about their children's health. And, most vivid is the picture of my father standing and speaking in churches and at camp meetings. He was persuasive, confident, and clear in his message. What strikes me now is his audience of African villagers, sitting, listening, and following every word, not distracted or bored, but intent. The words they were hearing had meaning in their lives beyond my young comprehension. But, I understand now.

How did this unusual understanding and bond come about between African villagers and white missionaries from the American Midwest? Often, missionaries withdrew into administrative isolation—or soon left Africa—following cultural conflicts, misunderstandings, and disillusionment. I believe part of my parents' success was that they listened. They learned the language and discovered a rich, sophisticated culture with a long, well-documented history. They were interested in all things

African. The Africans responded. I remember Pastor Joab Mulela, one of the early Christian pioneers in the Congo and still vigorous in his 70s, spending much time in our front room at Mulunguishi, instructing my father about what he could say or what he could do to present the gospel to Africans. My parents had very good teachers, and they listened.

One very important entre for outsiders to the central African culture was hunting. The Lunda and Luba were hunting tribes, committed to hunting for sport, food, and often to protect crops. Hunting in the southern Congo savannahs and forests was not easy and required skill, stamina, and courage. Hunting skill and the resultant stories provided a man's status and respect in the community and the tribe; indeed, in the province. My father—and my brother and I—took to this system with zeal and passion. When hunting in the bush, the problems of normal life were forgotten. It was a world of men, happy to be away from life's irritating duties and to be united in one thing: the hunt. Around campfires in hunting camps, there were no racial or cultural divides. And, it was here we came to know well the Africans with whom we hunted. We learned to admire their skills and character. Stories of my father's adventures with Cape buffalo charges, near tragedy with elephants, or his skill with a rifle spread quickly around the whole province and established his name and reputation. He was soon admired and respected. This hunting background helped him greatly in the conflicts and wars that came later. More importantly, he started to fully understand Africans.

What my parents learned in their first term in Africa changed them. My mother now focused on child evangelism and studied how to help women raise and care for their children. My father had been studying for a PhD in anthropology at the University of Hartford. After 1955, however, he halted his academic education and became practical. He took welding classes. He learned building techniques and carpentry. He focused on Bible study and evangelism. Later, he become expert in all areas of flying, from earning advanced flying ratings to rebuilding engines and airframes. He changed from building a resume that would promote his career to developing the skills, knowledge, and faith that would help the people he had come to serve and learned to love.

One central aspect of my parents' lives that is often obscured is this: what they started, they continued to the end. The same job. The same work. The same people. My father accepted no promotions. He did not climb any professional ladder. He did not become a bishop or a college professor or bureaucrat. In the 1970s, Lufthansa, a German airline with airfreight interests in Africa's mining sector, offered him a job as the Africa director of their freight service. They needed his aircraft skills, but also his language competency and knowledge of local conditions. His considerable political connections were also an asset. The pay offered was beyond generous. When he declined, they threw in a signing bonus that would have made him—bluntly—rich. They wanted him. Finally, they offered him extensive time off for missionary work "on the side." He refused this offer like many others. He told them that he was committed to God's work. He had started a job and would not leave it unfinished. Nor did he. Retirement came and went and still he continued without much regard for difficulty, age, or illness right up to the day of his death.

On June 8, 2006, my brother, John, called me from Africa and said that Dad's health was not good; that the end was approaching. I immediately called my father from my office and heard his cheerful voice ask how things were going at our factory. I replied that things were going well, but I was concerned about his health, and that his life was drawing to a close. He said, yes, he knew this was the case but was really more interested in talking about his fish ponds. He was watching over their construction at the Kafakumba Center. He described his outing in a golf cart that morning to see the progress of the excavations and dams being built. He was very pleased that the earth-moving equipment was making excellent progress. We discussed other aspects of the work in Congo, how mutual friends were doing, how church projects should be funded. Toward the end of the conversation, I said goodbye, and we calmly and without drama expressed our love for each other. He then said, "Oh, my students are here to sing for me." The African student pastors had come to sing for him. He loved African singing. He had a pleasant meal with his family, and later that night he died. Thus ended the great life of a good man: a faithful husband, a kind and wonderful father, and a brave, hardworking, servant of our Lord. He is buried at the Kafakumba Center next to his colleague Kasongo Munza, in Africa, where he belonged.

This book looks back on the lives of my parents and their colleagues who worked in the Congo. It also celebrates the 50 years of the Kafakumba Pastors' School and its mission and progress. But what about the future? What about the Pastors' School in the coming years? What about training successors for God's work in Central Africa? This book is part of an effort to see that the work of the Pastors' School does not end—that it continues and that God's work goes forward in the villages and towns in Central Africa and, ultimately, the world.

—Kenneth Nelson Enright

Sequence of Events

1922 (July 27)   Ken born to John and Ruth (Broomfield) Enright; Chicago, Illinois

1924 (Sept. 13)   Lorraine born to Nelson and Esther Farrier; Hillman, Michigan

1930 (Dec. 30)   Lorraine's father died

1931–1939   Lorraine's mother served as superintendent of schools

1940   Merlin joined the Navy

1942   Ken began studies at Taylor University in Upland, Indiana

1943   Lorraine started at Taylor University; she and Ken met there

1945 (May 23)   Ken graduated from Taylor University

1945 (May 26)   Ken and Lorraine were married in Hillman, Michigan

1945–1946   Ken attended Northern Baptist Seminary, Chicago

Ken and Lorraine served churches in Hamlet and Hanna, Indiana

1946–1948   Ken attended Asbury Seminary and Lorraine attended Asbury College; Ken pastored a church in New Vienna, Ohio

1946	Kenny Nelson born
1947	Lorraine graduated from Asbury College
1948	Ken graduated from Asbury Seminary
1948	Ken's missionary training at Kennedy School of Mission, Hartford, Connecticut (completed the first half of a Master's degree in Anthropology)
1949–1950	Ken and Lorraine undertook language training in Belgium
1950	John born
1950	The Enright family returned to US and then headed for Congo
1950–1955	Enright's assigned to Mulunguishi
1953	Elaine born in Likasi
1955	Family on furlough. Ken received his Master's degree from Kennedy School of Missions, Hartford, Connecticut
1955–1956	Family spent an additional year at Mulunguishi
1956–1966	Family assigned to Sandoa (Mwajinga) and Kafakumba
1958	Eileen born at Kapanga Hospital
1960	Family on furlough; Congo won independence from Belgium
1961	Enrights returned to Sandoa (Mwajinga) and Kafakumba. Ken started his flight ministry, Wings of the Morning, with Paul Alexander
1963	First Pastors' School held at Lake Kafakumba in Congo

1965	Elinda born at Kapanga Hospital
1965	Family on furlough
1966–1970	Enright's assigned to Lubumbashi and Kafakumba
1971	Furlough
1972–1978	Family was assigned to Kolweizi and Kafakumba
1978 (May)	Enright's held hostage in Kolweizi
1978–79	Family on furlough. Ken and Lorraine purchased a home in Florida
1980–1987	Enright's assigned to Manono in North Katanga Province and Kafakumba. Lorraine's mother came to live with them.
1981	Lorraine's mother died and was buried at Luena (the mission station of John and Kendra Enright)
1987	Ken and Lorraine began retirement. Although their primary home was in Florida, both Ken and Lorraine continued to return to Congo for Pastors' School and to oversee other projects.

Zambia

1998	Missionaries evacuated from Congo
1999	John purchased the property to build the Kafakumba Training Center, Zambia
2000	First Pastors' School held in Zambia
2006 (June 9)	Ken died and was buried at Kafakumba Training Center, Zambia

| 2013 | Lorraine continues her practice since retirement of spending her time divided between Florida and Africa (now Zambia) |
| | Nate and Elinda (Enright) Steury move to the Kafakumba Training Center, Zambia |

CHAPTER 1

The Early Years, 1922–1950

"Fear not, for I have redeemed you. I have called you by name; you are mine."

—Isaiah 43:1b

Lorraine, 1924–1943

The little girl's feet didn't even brush the floor as they swung back and forth beneath the bench on which she sat. This bench was no stranger to Lorraine; she almost lived in church—the Methodist Church of Hillman, Michigan—chosen because there was no Swedish Lutheran congregation in town. Her mother, Esther, was of Lutheran heritage (with a maiden name of Lundeen, one might guess so), but found the Methodist church entirely to her liking. Esther Christine Lundeen Farrier was a force to be reckoned with. Unusual in her day, Esther was college educated. Her marriage to the local Ford dealership owner and State Representative Nelson Grover Farrier meant that she enjoyed plentiful income, the elevated community status of the upper-middle class, and being an equal partner in marriage and parenting. Even when she was widowed in 1930 and had three small children—ages six, nine, and twelve—she taught school on a lifetime teaching certificate and worked as the superintendent of the Montmorency County Schools.

Esther adored Nelson. She catered to his every need, paying special attention to the meals she prepared to meet his required diabetic diet. Little Lorraine, still a preschooler, noted how these acts of food preparation and presentation were completed with such deep love and attention that she spent a lifetime emulating her mother's example. Beautiful dishes, wonderful food, good company, the joy of a shared meal—all became hallmarks of Lorraine's home, just as they had been in her childhood.

Nelson Farrier was a tall man, over six feet. Lorraine sometimes worried that she, too, might grow to be that tall. But, as her legs lengthened, and she could eventually touch the floor beneath the Methodist Church benches, she was relieved to reach a final height of five feet, four-and-one-half inches. Even so, because Lorraine was just six when her father died, she remembered him as a towering figure. Others remember him the same way. As chairman of the powerful Ways and Means Committee in the Michigan legislature and a popular local business owner, he had many friends. Even Henry Ford visited his Ford dealership in Hillman. Nelson loved politics, hunting, and fishing. He was a member of the Lincoln Club, a collection of wealthy Detroit businessmen who loved to hunt. His death in 1930 left many grieving friends, as well as his bereaved widow, Esther, and their three little children: Merlin (12 years old), Chester (9 years) and Lorraine (6 years). Even still, Lorraine remembers the pain of his death, the tears that poured from her broken heart, and the heartless question of a thoughtless adult who stooped and asked, "Why are you crying?" The pain of her own fatherlessness never left her.

There was one thing that cheered Esther: Nelson had made his peace with God before he died. Although Nelson had not attended church with her and the children, she knew that he had prayed and received a peace that comforted the family through their grief. Now, as never before, Esther poured herself into her family, work, and church. For 30 years, Esther was her church's Sunday school superintendent. She was known for staging elaborate drama and music programs, sometimes borrowing costuming from the local International Order of Odd Fellows lodge. The crowds were huge and packed the church to the gills. Lorraine continued to think of her mother as simply "on fire for the Lord," always serving, teaching, and helping others. Later, Esther remained a strong prayer supporter for Lorraine and her husband Ken's ministries in Congo. Fellow missionaries recognized Esther's role as she prayed for people in Congo, for her family's ministries there, for the growth and strength of a growing church in central Africa, and for the blessing of her daughter's family as they served in Congo. (1)

With Esther's devotion to the church, it was not surprising that Lorraine also found comfort in the activities of the church. "I was continuously nurtured in church from the time I was knee-high to a grasshopper," she remembered. "I always had a sense of God being with me. I loved the Lord from the moment I could breathe." Unlike her brothers, who didn't care to attend church when they were young (although later in life they also became very dedicated believers), she loved going to church and was always at her mother's side.

The Hillman Methodist Church was known for its evangelical fervor. Every year, evangelists came to town and held week-long revivals at the church. Closely tied to the conservative theology of Asbury Seminary in Kentucky, the revivals focused on a reverence for Scripture, repentance, and holiness in living. Lorraine soaked it in. Her excellent memory helped her learn large sections of the Bible by heart, and her competitive spirit drove her to become the annual champion at reading the most Bible verses before services. She was a girl with a tender heart who responded regularly to the pastors' altar calls. She was eight years old the year a missionary attended one of the Hillman revivals. When the woman asked if any felt called to be a missionary, Lorraine felt a stirring in her heart and raised her hand.

From then on, Lorraine had a sense of God's purpose and leading in her life. She believed she would be a missionary.

It was no surprise that Lorraine inherited a lively intelligence and quick wit from her parents. She was always an ambitious student, telling herself rather continually that, "I am going to be number one. And I was," she remembered years later, "except for algebra, which just got me down in school." Her dream was to attend Taylor University in Upland, Indiana, after graduating from high school. But family circumstances and a world at war delayed her dream for a couple of years.

Brothers Merlin and Chester had graduated by this time and moved away from home. The early 40s were a time of war, so Merlin joined the United States Navy and was serving in Japan within months of when Lorraine graduated from high school. Chester had attended Taylor University earlier, but family circumstances changed when a fire swept through their extensive landholdings, and he returned to Hillman to salvage as much timber from the land as possible. The task's urgency pushed him to start the Farrier Lumber Company, later to be joined in business by his mother. When war came in 1941, he wanted to follow his brother into military service, but a hole in his eardrum barred him from joining the Army.

Meanwhile, in 1941, Lorraine remained in Hillman after high school graduation to help her mother and continue her own education closer to home at the County Normal College. Two years later, she received a teaching certificate and taught in a rural school for $25 a month. Teaching every grade level in the tiny one-room school was the best preparation she ever had for her lifetime of work, Lorraine believed. With Chester back in Hillman and settling into the community, Lorraine felt free to pursue her dream of attending Taylor University.

And so, in the late summer of 1943 Lorraine left Hillman to begin classes at Taylor. She did not know that within that first week she would meet a fellow student named Ken Enright, and her life would change forever.

Endnote

1. Esther Farrier was known by many for her Christian witness and habits of prayer. Lena Eschtruth, a fellow missionary in Congo, attributed much of Ken and Lorraine Enright's success in their lifelong ministry in Congo to the prayers of Lorraine's mother. "She was praying for them all the time," Lena later said. "She bathed all of their lives and work in prayer, and it made a difference. Many times it's not just what you see, but the prayer going on behind the scenes, that really matters," Lena continued. Elinda Enright Steury, Ken and Lorraine's youngest daughter, also believed in the power of her grandmother's prayers, believing that her grandmother had prayed her future husband, Nate Steury, right into her life. "She was such a wonderful woman of faith. She was great," remembered Elinda. Not only have Elinda and Nate been life partners in ministry, but they are now planning to return to their beloved Africa to provide leadership at Kafakumba Pastors' School. Indeed, Esther Lundeen Farrier's prayers were powerful during her lifetime, and they also continue to have far-reaching effects today.

Ken, 1922–1942

The Enright family name was well-known on Chicago's Southside; it still is in some circles of the city's Irish-Democrat-Union political machine. John J. and Ruth (Broomfield) lived on 80th Street in the early years of the 20th Century. John's day job was working as a milkman for Bowman Dairy, a job that took him to the front porches of many Southside families. At the same time, he worked his way up in the Teamsters Union, where he became influential in Teamsters politics. His efforts to unionize workplaces ensured that not only did he make a fair living, but many other families were helped during the Great Depression. Lorraine said it this way: "He fed many other families during the Great Depression. It was such a blessing." Ruth stayed at home and cared for the eight children that filled their home. Chicago's Southside was a rough neighborhood, known for hard fists, corner bars, large families, and the dockyards of Lake Michigan's southern shores.

Ken Enright was born July 27, 1922, third in a line of children that included oldest sister Elizabeth, second-in-line brother

Jack, and followed by Ruth Ellen, Delores, Janie, Roger, and Bobby. He was close to his mother, "…just so especially close," Lorraine recalled. So close, that at times she relied on his quick wit to ensure that John's paycheck made it home from the dairy on time. A favorite family story maintained that Ruth sent Ken to the local bar on pay day to find his father and hurry him on home before drinking away the family paycheck. Ken would go into the bar, and his dad would buy him a plate of food to keep the child occupied and leave him alone with his beer and circle of friends. Ken, however, would knock his plate over and urge his father to leave with him before the bartender could raise a ruckus over the spilled food. It worked every time, according to family legend, and Ken was well on his way to developing his quick wits, fast thinking, and charm that remained lifetime traits.

Ruth Broomfield Enright came from a Christian Science home, but she attended and grew to love the Ingleside Methodist Church on Chicago's Southside. Her children accompanied her to church, so Ken remembered attending Sunday school as a child and Methodist Youth Fellowship as a teen. Ken liked to regale later audiences with stories about his growing up as a "street tough" in the neighborhoods of Chicago's Southside. His gritty upbringing gave Ken an uncanny common sense and street-smart abilities that came into good stead throughout his adult years. Living in a home with a large family, surrounded by friends and his father's union associates, and scrapping out a life in a tough Irish neighborhood meant that Ken also perfected his people skills. "All his life," Lorraine emphasized over and over again, "he was just so good with people. He really knew how to get along with people." Perhaps this is an understatement, considering the extraordinary network of friends, family, and supporters that surrounded Ken during his lifetime. Extraordinary, too, was his ability to gauge his relationships constantly, develop new ones and rely on old ones. This quality saved many lives during his years in Africa.

After graduating from high school in 1940, Ken attended Wilson Junior College, but quit to work on the docks and barges of Lake Michigan's southern shores, dredging the drainage canals throughout Chicago. Having grown up near the Lake he was an outstanding swimmer, whose skills were appreciated by the captain of his barge. By his late teens, Ken had long since stopped attending church with his mother. He was handsome and strong and enjoyed the pleasures of youthful indiscretions. In later years he often said of his youth that he "was a smart-aleck tough." He was skilled with a deck of cards, too, and known for winning money from his fellow deck hands at their regular gambling table. His life—and his habits—caught the eye of the Swedish captain on the barge, who kept telling him he should be "born again." Ken would swear at him, but one time the words caught up with him.

Ken's conversion still remains a mystery to Lorraine and to others in his life. But Ken Enright's transformation from a man with a promising political and union career to a man of God seemed immediate, profound, and intense. He was a young man with a wide-open future, whose Irish Teamsters Union politics could have opened doors to anything he wanted. But it was not to be, and his fellow card players on the dredging barge were as surprised as anybody.

By all accounts, it had been an ordinary day when the group sat down to play a game of poker. Ken won the game and the money that went with the winning. Rather than sticking around the break room, Ken climbed a masthead and thought about the Captain's words. He pondered the idea of starting again with a clean slate; indeed, of being born again. Perhaps he remembered the constant nurturing and experiences at Ingleside Church, his mother's love and admonishments, the misery of his father's drinking. Perhaps he was convicted of his own sin and need for forgiveness and a new beginning. Nobody really knows.

Later he told people that he looked at the lights of the city and acknowledged that he was "finished." He went on to pray, "Lord, give me a second chance." Whatever the weight on his conscience, that day was the turning point in Ken's young life. He told his shipmates of his decision to follow God, left his poker money on the table, and walked away from the waterfront. Lorraine later remarked that she did not, and would never, know what happened. For her, Ken's conversion was as sudden and mysterious as the Apostle Paul's blinding on the road to Damascus. In fact, Paul became one of her favorite Biblical apostles, and one to whom she could compare not only Ken's conversion, but also his lifetime commitment to serving God as a missionary in foreign places.

Immediately after his masthead conversion, Ken felt called to be a minister. His sister Elizabeth's husband had gone to Taylor University, so Ken was influenced to attend there too. Yet Ken struggled with his desire to leave home and go to school. He wondered how he could ever be effective in his call to ministry while his father remained an unbeliever. But God gave him the peace that others would influence his family while he devoted himself to his studies. This belief later came true with the conversion of his father and other family members.

In 1942, Ken hitchhiked to Upland, Indiana and spent his first year at Taylor exploring what he believed was his call to ministry. Always known to be a hard worker, Ken not only went to school but also worked in steel fabrication factories and paid his way through school. In addition, he pastored a church. Upon arriving at Taylor, he called on the district superintendent of local Methodist churches and announced that he wanted to be a minister.

Soon he found himself the student pastor of a small congregation now called Mount Olive United Methodist Church, which he later called "the best training for mission I ever had." Mount Olive was a country church—even requiring that Ken take care of the pot-bellied stove and be the building janitor— but its farm families surrounded their city-boy minister with a lot of love. One of the church's parishioners remembered arriving at the church one day and finding the door locked. It was not a problem for Ken, who pulled out an old skill and promptly picked the lock. "Those old farmers taught me more about the Lord than any school or university I've ever been to," he liked to say. "They taught me what living by faith meant." He loved the congregation at Mount Olive, and they loved him too, begging him to stay on as their pastor when his schooling finished. "One farmer even promised to give him a farm if he would just stay," remarked Lorraine.

The young ladies at Taylor and Mount Olive all noticed the handsome new minister with the charismatic personality. Some would ask to be taken to his church, even asking the young man out. But Ken remained steadfast in his goal to dedicate his first year at school to figuring out God's call for his life. At some point in those early days at Taylor, a missionary to Angola, John Wengatz, visited the campus and spoke to the student body during chapel. His challenge to serve God as a missionary fell on an open heart, and Ken felt the Spirit move in him once again. He would have bounded up to the altar to confirm the call, but he knew that kneeling there would have made the holes in his shoes evident to others. So again, alone with God—this time in his tiny room in a student dormitory—he said yes to the powerful leading of the Holy Spirit in his life.

Ken entered his second year at Taylor University confirmed in his call to ministry and sensing a direction toward ministry in the central African country called Belgian Congo. Just before fall classes started, he stopped by the campus book store to purchase books for the semester. He had also just been invited to meet the Chancellor and other staff and professors at a formal event held at the beginning of each school year.

Lorraine

Lorraine had settled into her room when she arrived on campus but had yet to purchase her books for the start of classes the following week. She stopped at the campus bookstore and began looking for the needed titles, only to be approached by a young man who invited her to attend a formal reception with him that Friday evening. Out of the blue. Unexpected. In recalling the encounter, Lorraine smiled, and a twinkle lit her eyes as she remembered what he looked like: "Tall, dark, and handsome, with curly hair." At 6'2" and handsome as an Irish morning, Ken made an impression. Lorraine said yes. "I bowled him over with my white formal that evening," she laughed. Was it love at first sight? Lorraine insisted no; they dated for a year before deciding to marry, and both knew that each felt a serious call on their lives to serve God. "But I had mine first," said Lorraine, as she recalled the missionary who had challenged her when she was just eight years old to give her life to God. And, she did.

School Years: 1943–1950

Lorraine fit right into Ken's life as pastor and student. She grew up attending church and felt entirely at home at Mount Olive Methodist. Her nursing studies took up most of her time, but that was okay, because dating rules were very strict at Taylor. "We could walk to the post office to get the mail," she remembered, "and we were allowed only one hour together on weeknights. On weekends we had to be in by a 10 o'clock curfew." They spent what time they could together; Ken's work, studies, and pastorate made that time limited and precious. Ken later confessed to friends that he really wouldn't have amounted to much if he hadn't met Lorraine. Lorraine's strong faith helped him find his own, and her high expectations for the man she would marry were always centered in his willingness to attend church and prayer meetings. "I saw how hard it was that my father didn't go to church with my mother, and so I decided that whomever I married would have to do that," explained Lorraine.

The two continued to see each other. One year later, during their summer break in August, Ken made a trip to Michigan and asked Lorraine to marry him. Perhaps it was the memories of his childhood on Lake Michigan or a premonition of the beautiful Lake Kafakumba of his future that caused Ken to propose at a favored shore on Lake Avalon. Lorraine was happy to beat her brother, Chester, to the punch when she announced her engagement at a large family dinner. Chester was not to be outdone, and soon he was engaged to Dorothy McReady, Lorraine's best friend. The two couples began making plans for a double wedding.

Lorraine loved Dorothy like a sister, and the two remained very close all the years of their lives—"a friend to the end," she liked to say. "Dorothy loved our children just as much as her own," Lorraine later recalled. "Every year we were in Africa she sent my girls the most b-e-a-u-t-i-f-u-l dresses; you just can't imagine." The Farrier Lumber business was good to Chester and Dorothy, and they were generous supporters of Ken and Lorraine's work and their family for many years. Lorraine admired Dorothy's grit and spirit right through her old age: "She was feisty and had an obsession to care for herself; she was an independent woman who did not want to rely on her children for her well-being." Probably the two were equal in grit and determination, making for a fine family friendship that endured well.

Lorraine's engagement to Ken meant that she had to abandon her pursuit of a nursing degree; unfortunately, married students were not allowed to study nursing at Taylor during those years. Instead, Lorraine focused on education during her junior year at Taylor—an education she later recalled as having cost $1,000.

On May 23, 1945, Ken graduated from Taylor University; on May 26th, he and Lorraine were married in Hillman. Although Ken wanted to attend Asbury Seminary in Wilmore, Kentucky to earn his theological degree, the school was not yet approved as a seminary for Methodist pastors. So Ken and Lorraine moved to "a little, tiny room in the lowest of low places in Chicago" so that Ken could study at Northern Baptist Seminary. (The Seminary was located in the inner city, which explains Lorraine's memory of the tiny room they shared there.) During their year of study, Ken was assigned to pastor two small Methodist churches in Hamlet and Hannah, both located in northwestern Indiana.

During that year at Northern Baptist, Asbury received its accreditation as a Methodist Seminary, and the newlyweds made plans for Ken to transfer. In the fall of 1946, the two moved to Kentucky for Ken's two years of seminary training. (Asbury Seminary has deep roots in the teachings of John Wesley, Methodism's founder. It is widely known for its strong support of global ministry, a conservative approach to Biblical scholarship, and remains the choice for many Methodist ministers in the Midwest.) He also accepted appointment to a pastorate in New Vienna, Ohio, which meant many long hours on the road every weekend travelling the 300 miles back and forth. Always known for being hard workers, Ken and Lorraine juggled their studies with leading a church, including the children's and youth activities. The two held kids' craft classes for Child Evangelism every Saturday evening, led the Sunday worship services, and worked with youth on Sunday evenings. On Monday morning they headed back to school at Wilmore.

Always the entrepreneur, Ken stopped and picked up peaches on these weekend trips and took them back to sell to fellow students at Wilmore. Out of season, he did the same thing with varied wholesale items, purchasing them en route and selling to buyers in small towns in Kentucky. The couple's first car, a Ford purchased with $1,000 of Lorraine's tuition money, provided bare-bones transportation, and its lack of a heater made winter travel with a new baby an ordeal. They traded it in for a Mercury, a car that Lorraine called "a real, real blessing." She credited it with her and Ken's ability to commute thousands of miles between Wilmore and New Vienna.

During the fall semester of their first year at Asbury, Ken and Lorraine welcomed their first child to the family: Kenneth Nelson. Kenny was born in the parsonage at New Vienna and adapted well to his parents' frenetic lives. After two years at Asbury, both his parents had attained their degrees: Ken had earned his Master's Degree in Divinity in 1948, and Lorraine the year before with her Bachelor's Degree in Philosophy and Religion. Like all the other churches they served, New Vienna wanted Ken to stay as their permanent minister, but the two had their eyes set on Africa; Congo to be exact.

The call to ministry and serving God as missionaries had been clear to both of them. At eight years old, Lorraine gave her life to mission service at a church camp near Romeo, Michigan. The missionary speaker that week had returned recently from Asia; her colorful clothing and vibrant message remained clear in Lorraine's mind for a lifetime. Ken had been challenged by John and Helen Wengatz during his years at Taylor University. Their passion for Angola and other countries in Central Africa left a powerful impression on Ken. As such, when the mission agency of the Methodist Church came to Asbury—just before Ken and Lorraine graduated—looking for people to go to Africa, the two decided to move forward with applying for mission service.

The Methodist Church had experienced very lean years during the Great Depression and World War II. Work that had started decades earlier by pioneering missionaries in Congo, John (later a bishop) and Helen Springer, had been cut back or turned over to African leadership. Many of the earliest missionaries were unable to tolerate the conditions in Congo—malaria and tropical illnesses took many lives; others returned to the United States because of chronic medical conditions or schooling for their children. After World War II, however, interest in Methodist work in Congo was renewed—along with new drugs to prevent and treat the deadly diseases encountered there. Ken and Lorraine met with the Bishop of Congo and then joined a new group of post-World War II applicants for service. They were accepted immediately and sent to Hartford, Connecticut for a year of study at the Kennedy School of Missions before being assigned to work in Central Congo. During that year, they attended a small German Methodist church. In later years, Ken referred to his years of education at Northern Baptist Seminary, Asbury Seminary, and Kennedy Theological Seminary this way:

"A Calvinist, a Holiness, and a liberal school—I did it on purpose. I didn't want to be captivated by any seminary. I took what I wanted from each…You have to face things from all sides."

After eight years of school, the two were finally nearing their goal. Only one year remained: language study in Brussels, Belgium. Because Congo was a Belgian colony and French-speaking country, the two were required to learn the language before leaving for Africa. It meant packing up little Kenny and sailing across the Atlantic on a World War II troop transport called the *Marine Thresher*. Lorraine remembers the ocean journey as "the most horrible trip I've ever taken." She and Ken were separated for the crossing, with Ken assigned to the D deck down in the hull of the ship. She and three-year-old Kenny were assigned to the higher B deck with other women and children, a life-saving move if the ship were to hit any leftover wartime explosives. She missed not being together and suffered from the separation during their days at sea. The ocean crossing was the first of many for the little family in the ensuing years but was perhaps the most symbolic. Ken and Lorraine left the United States uncertain about both the journey and their destination, but were firm in their belief that theirs was a journey God had planned. They never wavered and never lost faith that they were always led by God and kept safe in His keeping. At their wedding, they sang the hymn, "Savior Like a Shepherd Lead Us"; its words remained written in their hearts long after the music faded. (1)

Eventually, they arrived in Antwerp and took a train to Brussels to begin their studies. Post-war Belgium was a depressing place. Bombed-out sectors remained unrepaired from the ravages of World War II; the Belgians were poor, and food was scarce. Lorraine remembered Belgium as a cloudy, rainy, and dismal place. "I don't know why anyone would want to live in Belgium, nobody would choose it," she said many years later. "It had a terrible climate, and it rained all the time. If you like rain and cold, you'd love it," she added for emphasis.

The Mission Board had not arranged housing for the little family, so they had to find a place suitable for their one-year stay. It was not easy, but they managed to find a fully-furnished, second-floor apartment. "It was not up to American styles, but it would certainly do," Lorraine recalled. They had no refrigerator, so kept their food cold in an old packing box on their little balcony. "Belgium was such a cold country we got along fine with that," she continued. They also had a little gas stove in the kitchen…with the emphasis on "little" for its size, but "big" for the mess it was in. "That stove was such a big mess, you wouldn't even use it on a camping trip," exclaimed Lorraine.

Both Ken and Lorraine excelled in their studies. "Ken had a gift for languages and learned quickly; I also managed just fine," Lorraine remembered. It was no small feat learning a new language in a new country, especially when the family welcomed child number two, John Jay, in the spring of 1950. While Lorraine was in the hospital giving birth, they were notified of a change in their African assignment: The Mission Board was sending them to Southern rather than Central Congo. "We looked at each other while I was lying in the hospital with our new son and said, 'We don't know either place. We'll be glad to go wherever you feel we are most needed.'" Later, Lorraine was very thankful they had not been sent to Central Congo, where the effects of the wars after Independence were much harsher. "The missions and missionaries collapsed so quickly in that area. I was so glad we were in South Katanga."

The two finished their year of language study, returned to the United States, and quickly prepared to go to Congo. With two little boys in tow, one just three months old, Ken and Lorraine spent what time they could with family before beginning their journey to Africa.

Ken had one piece of unfinished business before leaving. He was troubled about his own call to Africa while believing that many in his own family needed to know God. During Ken's years away studying, Billy Graham held several large crusades at Soldier's Field in Chicago. Many of his family members responded to Christ at these crusades, beginning with his mother's new commitment and eventually his father's. Ken and Lorraine were excited to see so many members of his family become outstanding Christians. His father's life was transformed from one of drinking to one of devotion to faith and family. "He was just so good to me," Lorraine remembered of Ken's father. Their newfound faith so permeated the family that it produced two missionaries to Africa: Ken's nephew, Lowell Wurtz (son of sister, Ruth Ellen) became a missionary to Congo and continues to work in Tanzania with his wife Claudia.

Endnote

1. Lorraine considered their wedding hymn "Savior Like a Shepherd Lead Us" as her favorite song throughout her life. Its words were an apt reflection of the One she chose to follow all of her life, as well as a guide for how she and Ken chose to live their lives. They literally lived the words with which they sealed their wedding vows.

"Savior Like a Shepherd Lead Us" by Dorothy A. Thrupp

> *"... That great shepherd of the sheep... make you perfect in every good work.*

-Hebrews 13:20-21

1. Savior like a Shepherd lead us, much we need Thy tender care;
    In Thy pleasant pastures feed us; for our use Thy folds prepare.
    Blessed Jesus, blessed Jesus, Thou hast bought us, Thine we are;
    Blessed Jesus, Blessed Jesus, Thou has bought us, Thine we are.
2. We are Thine, do Thou befriend us; be the guardian of our way;
    Keep Thy flock from sin, defend us; Seek us when we go astray.
    Blessed Jesus, Blessed Jesus, Hear Thy children when they pray;
    Blessed Jesus, Blessed Jesus, Hear Thy children when they pray.
3. Early let us seek Thy favor; early let us do Thy will;
    Blessed Lord and only Savior, with Thy love our bosoms fill.
    Blessed Jesus, Blessed Jesus, Thou has loved us, love us still;
    Blessed Jesus, Blessed Jesus, Thou has loved us, love us still.
    Amen.

Ken and Lorraine on their wedding day, May 26, 1945 with (l to r): Ken's father, John Enright; Lorraine's mother, Esther Farrier; and at far right, Ken's mother, Ruth Enright.

Ken and Lorraine began their missionary work studying French in Brussels, Belgium. With toddler Kenny in tow and John born during language study, 1950 gave them an early taste of their many years of balancing family and ministry duties.

CHAPTER 2

Mulungwishi, 1950–1956

"You did not choose me, but I chose you and appointed you to go and bear fruit—fruit that will last."

—John 15:16a

Back on a ship again—this time together, at least—Ken and Lorraine re-crossed the Atlantic in two weeks on the *President Cartier*. It was no luxury ocean liner, but a cargo ship that carved out space for 12 passengers, the Enrights being four of them. Lorraine remembered the crossing as difficult: she washed diapers for three-month old John the whole way, and the ship encountering a terrible storm. They were greeted in Matadi, a port on the Congo River, by Swedish missionaries who gave them dinner and a welcomed respite while their ship was being unloaded. Matadi, however, provided no access to southern Congo, so the family re-boarded the ship and travelled down the coast to Lubito Bay, Angola. There they stayed with a missionary family until they could find a train to take them to Congo; train travel was the only way to reach their ultimate destination.

Lorraine remembered the train trip well. They boarded the Benguela Railway for a journey of 1,400 miles into the heart of

Africa. They moved slowly, about 15 miles per hour, and stopped often to pick up wood and water for the engine's firebox. "Burning embers from the train, still hot and glowing, often flew through the windows and burned holes in our clothes," she remembered. The burning embers also sometimes set fire to the grass and forests along the tracks. They travelled along the timeworn passage of Angola and Central Africa's slave trading history. Lorraine recalled seeing people in chains, prisoners working on the railway, and witnessing "awful, just awful, things being done to others." It was her first introduction to African life—and it was a long way from her home in the Midwest. The family changed trains at the Congo border and finally arrived at their first mission station in the town of Mulungwishi. It was three in the morning.

"We had a little Belgian buggy for Johnny, but we had no idea how we would get all of our things unloaded from the train and transported to our new home," she said. The family was exhausted. Fortunately, a group of Africans were awaiting their arrival, and soon the resident missionaries-in-charge descended a hill to greet them. Doris and Elwood (Woody) Bartlett made them feel welcome and helped them to their home.

Housing was in short supply around the station, but the Bartletts had fixed up a building that had once been used as a carpenter shop. It was simple and furnished with cast-offs from the mission station—including hospital beds for sleeping. "The beds were tall," Lorraine remembered. "One night I couldn't find my baby, John. I was hunting all over for him and was getting desperate. Well, he had rolled into the mosquito netting and just rolled right under that tall hospital bed but was not hurt in any way," Lorraine recalled. One year later, the family moved up the hill, joining other missionary families in the larger compound. "I loved our house at Mulungwishi," Lorraine remembered. "It had a fireplace that we painted white, and all the rooms were painted in different colors. I always tried to keep a nice home—not necessarily American style, but nice." Fireplaces in homes were very practical, providing the only warmth the family had during the cool season (the altitudes of the Katanga Plateau meant many chilly mornings and evenings). As the family grew, Lorraine remembered lighting fires many times when the children developed malaria. "They would be so sick in the morning, and I'd build a fire while they lay around. By noon they'd be running around like nothing was wrong."

Ken and Lorraine were put right to work in Mulungwishi. Ken was named the district missionary (something akin to a district superintendent) under the American Bishop of Congo, Newell Booth. Bishop Booth was known for his great love of the people in growing village churches, and he supported Ken's desire to get out of the city among the rural people. Ken visited many of the district's little churches, getting to know the pastors and people in surrounding regions, and preaching in different communities weekly. He also taught school at the local high school, the Ecole de Moniteur. The big surprise for Ken and Lorraine when they arrived was that they were expected to learn Swahili immediately. Lorraine found learning the new language to be "very, very hard—I just about died," especially so quickly after learning French. But both learned the tribal language and continued to be fluent in both languages of the region. Ken preached in Swahili and worked with local pastors in that language, but taught school in French.

In addition to caring for two little boys and learning Swahili, Lorraine taught in the Women's School and helped prepare food. She also taught children and, later, the wives of students attending the Methodist high school and college. "We taught the women how to read and write; they had not been to school and had no idea where to even start. We started right where they were with just songs and other things. They wrote lessons on a slate." Lorraine remembered every student who attended the high school at Mulungwishi, but one girl in particular remained vivid. Unfortunately, she also remembered that the girl became pregnant and gave birth a few weeks before graduation. Being 1954, a time with different policies, the girl was not allowed to graduate. Lorraine taught in the Women's School for all of their six years at Mulungwishi, after which the school was turned over to an African administration. Mulungwishi proved to be the beginning of what became Lorraine's life-long passion of working with young women.

When other missionaries returned to the United States on furlough, Ken and Lorraine jumped in to continue their work. It meant that Ken found himself not only a district superintendent, missionary, and teacher, but also an evangelist out preaching each week and head of the Mulungwishi mission farm. Two missionaries, Maurice Persons and Woody Bartlett, asked Ken if he would help with the preliminary work of starting a theological seminary while they returned to the States for a year of furlough. Ken tackled the task with gusto and soon had a preliminary structure in place. Son John clearly remembered those early classes held in the basement of their home. Although only three at the time, he remembered the windows, the chalkboard, the small group of African pastor/students, and his father's figure as he taught the group in his newly-learned Swahili, which he considered better than his also newly-acquired French. The school, which became the life-work of fellow missionaries Woody Bartlett and Maurice Persons, was founded in 1951, becoming the Faculte Methodiste de Theologie—The Mulungwishi Methodist Theological Seminary.

The Methodist Church was a thriving denomination before the mid-century missionaries arrived. Actually, the Congolese were a very receptive audience to Christianity, even centuries before when early Portuguese priests and other European emissaries entered the country. Early Methodist missionaries arriving at the turn of the 19th and 20th centuries had good success establishing churches and schools. But it was their own initiative and passion for God that spurred the growth of Congolese churches and their need for pastors. When Ken and Lorraine arrived in Congo in 1950, they entered a country of actively growing churches, many without pastors, and many Congolese wanting and needing to be trained to lead congregations. The Seminary at Mulingwishi was a response to this obvious need. Today, it continues training a national clergy for the fast-growing number of churches in the country, especially in the Katanga Province.

Southern Congo proved to be a pleasant place to live. The great Katanga Plateau stretches across southern Congo, rising to heights of 4,500' to 6,000', which creates a sunny temperate climate year-round. Having been raised in Michigan and after enduring a gloomy year in Belgium, Lorraine welcomed the sunshine.

Three years after arriving at Mulungwishi, Elaine was born in the mining hospital of the neighboring town of Jadotville (now Likasi), 25 miles away. The growing family thrived at the mission station. The children were healthy and played with the children of other missionaries as well as the children of Congolese pastors and friends. The Bartletts and Persons, other young missionary families, had children close in age to Kenny, John, and Elaine, and they still have many memories of their times together. All three children also had close African friends. Elaine found a best friend in a pastor's daughter; her name was Jenny Chiwengo. Elaine and Jenny played house and dolls, but with an African twist: Lorraine would make a little fire outside for them to cook over. As the two played house, cooking over their outdoor fire, one wonders how the two brought their very different worlds together into their daily play.

Lorraine vividly remembered an incident involving some of the African children on the station. One day a group of older children were cutting the grass with traditional kupwes, sharp metal blades about three feet long. One lad was cutting away somewhat slowly. "He looked half asleep," said Lorraine. "Suddenly, a little antelope jumped up out of the grass." Instantly, the boy's hunter instinct emerged and he dashed full-speed after the antelope, killing it and taking it home. He sang *God Bless Africa* all the way at the top of his lungs.

The family learned three languages and spoke them fluently—fluently enough that when little John was bitten one day by a scorpion, he screamed out in Swahili—"alinipika"—so that not only his mother, but other children, would know his plight. That incident remained a vivid memory for Lorraine who admitted to being terrified that day of the scorpion bite. Two-year-old John had stuck his foot into his shoe where the scorpion lurked; fortunately, the spider was small and caused pain, but no lasting damage. The children became so fluent that when they left for furlough in the United States, Kenny and John plotted to speak only Swahili on their arrival. They were going to pretend that they had forgotten how to speak English while living in Africa.

Mealtime was an important time in the Enright household. Lorraine had learned well from her mother the importance of good food and a grand table. Fortunately, she had kitchen help throughout her years in Africa. Her first Congolese cook, Norbert, was a great cook and very kind. He had wonderful culinary skills and was pleasant company for the family. However, every once in a while Norbert would go off and get drunk—a habit of which Methodist missionaries didn't approve. So, Lorraine had to let him go. Norbert's response to her goodbye tears stuck with her for a lifetime: "Don't cry Mama (the African term for the woman of a house). We Africans walk awhile, and then we fall awhile." Lorraine never did learn if he managed to stop drinking.

Some missionaries maintained a mostly American lifestyle while in Congo; the Enrights maintained both—an easygoing, somewhat Africanized household blended with strictly-held American customs. The family always had morning devotions together, generally using *The Upper Room* (a Methodist publication) or the Bible. Lorraine sent her children off in the morning with a hug and a prayer. Evenings brought another short devotional after supper. Friday night was always Family Night, an evening of family games and special food. Ken's very playful personality made Friday nights a lot of fun, and other children on the station were often invited to join them for the activities.

The family tried to eat breakfast and supper together, and Lorraine kept simple, but familiar foods on the table. She was adamant, however, about maintaining the high standards she had learned from her mother whenever guests joined them. "When the Bishop came, I really put on the dog," she smiled. She was known for a special egg dish she made for breakfast and for a wide variety of special desserts. Like her missionary friend, Doris Davis, she baked quite profusely. "When you came to one of our homes for a meal, you knew you'd been out. Others weren't that way, but that was okay."

For Lorraine, baking was an important way to maintain the traditions of home. "I baked my own bread, cakes, and cookies, and everything was done from scratch." The family enjoyed homemade cinnamon rolls for breakfast every Sunday morning. Although Lorraine enjoyed doing most of her own cooking, it was never easy. She constantly battled keeping bugs out of the ingredients or ants away from finding the fresh-baked goods. One family remembered ants invading a beautifully baked cake Lorraine had made for company. She tried picking them off the frosting, but finally gave up in despair. "Eat 'em, they're clean bugs," she declared. All this cooking required boiling water, sometimes ordering ingredients months ahead from far off places, and was done on a kitchen stove that burned wood, supplemented only occasionally using a gas stove (while living in the bush) or by an electric stove in their city homes.

"We always kept chickens in Mulungwishi," Lorraine remembered. One Sunday afternoon she went out to the coop and found that a snake had gotten into the chicken house and eaten the freshly laid eggs. She continued, "We saw the snake come out, and we saw the four eggs clearly inside it. We killed the snake, took the eggs—still in their shells—out of it, and put them back under the chickens. The chickens never rejected those eggs. We were so surprised that it worked!"

Although the family ate simply, they enjoyed much greater variety than their Congolese neighbors. The staple food for the region was bukadi (sometimes referred to as bukati or bukari in different regions), a thick porridge made from starchy flour pounded from the roots of the cassava, or manioc, plant. The cassava plant takes three years to mature, sometimes growing thick and sometimes thin. When mature, the roots are dug up, soaked for three days (in a local river or stream) and then left to dry in the sun on mats. Soaking was required because the roots were poisonous if eaten before being soaked and pounded. When the roots were dry, the women and children pounded them into flour with heavy wooden mortars. Children disliked the job because it gave them blisters before their hands became accustomed to the motions. Women developed beautiful rhythms while pounding, singing in their dance-like circles with mortar in hand. Sometimes, the flour was mixed with an equal part of corn flour. Lorraine liked cassava flour when it was mixed with corn, but the locals preferred a pure cassava. A similar mixture could be found in surrounding countries; although those to the south favored corn flour (bukadi was similar to the corn porridges known as nshima in Zambia and sadza in Zimbabwe, for example). The bukadi was thick enough to be broken off and rolled into small balls with one hand while eaten. It was generally served with fried greens (pumpkin leaves, rapeseed, or other greens) and pounded peanuts. Occasionally, meat (chicken or antelope were common) would be added to the mixture, perhaps with tomatoes, and referred to as a "relish." For people living along rivers and lakes, fish was an important staple in their diet.

Ken and Lorraine's early years on the field were ones of much listening and learning. Theirs was not only an experience of adjusting to another culture, but of becoming immersed into and developing an affinity with that culture. Fortunately, many guides surrounded them, especially among the Congolese pastors. Several became lifelong friends, confidants, and advisors. Their friendship and advice helped bridge the yawning gap between the American and African cultures. It would take years of listening and learning and continual effort to understand the people with whom they were called to serve. However, there is no doubt that it was those long periods spent in villages, hunting trips, and careful listening to their African colleagues that made the biggest impact on their ministries.

Mulungwishi also gave them an early taste for both the joy and the heartache that would become their life of Africa. Ken rarely wrote about the many difficult situations they faced, but in an early letter home he wrote to his family "I'm not called to publish the message of sin. Newspapers do that. I'm called to publish the Lord Jesus Christ who can save us from our sins, and that's all I want to do. The next time I write that we've been busy, remember that that doesn't necessarily mean teaching classes or building churches."

Six years passed quickly as Ken and Lorraine began the work that would continue for a lifetime: evangelistic services, preaching, teaching, camp meetings, leadership, and education—all established their roots at Mulungwishi. Over time, other work emerged and more children were born. In 1955, the family returned to the United States for a year of continued education, speaking in churches, and family renewal. Ken finished his Master's degree in Anthropology at the Kennedy School of Mission on this first furlough.

A Typical Day

Rarely was one day like another in Congo. Ken and Lorraine worked in so many different areas of ministry that each day and each person and situation that entered their lives was different. They never knew who would come to their door, and people were at their back door day and night. They never knew what message would come across the radio or what emergency would send Ken into the air for rescue. (Ken earned his pilot's license and founded an aviation ministry a few short years after they left Mulungwishi.) They never knew how the day's uncertainty would resolve or what might happen at a school, church, dispensary, or day-care for which they were responsible. Then again, they lived in a country that changed its name six times during the years they lived there.

Of two things they were certain: God's presence with them and the constant uncertainty on the road ahead of them.

However, elements of each day were similar. Because both were involved in teaching, they prepared lessons and spent time with students. After Ken began flying (Wings of the Morning became the name of flight ministry in Congo), radio network time with other stations and flight following were always part of the day. Lorraine recalled a typical day at both a city and a bush site: Mulungwishi, the city of their first assignment, and the bush of Sandoa, their second assignment.

A typical day in the city (Mulungwishi):

6 a.m.: Up with the sun for a breakfast of oat-meal, toast, and the ever-present local papaya. Milk was the powdered variety, and the adults enjoyed coffee (Nescafe) or tea. Meals required a lot of preparation because fruits and vegetables were fresh. Milk was purchased annually at Likasi— 316 cans for the year. In the early years, water had to be hauled up from the river in barrels and left undisturbed for two days to rid it of bilharzia (parasitic worms found in fresh water), followed by a good boiling. Later, large barrels were filled with water and gravity fed to faucets in the house. After breakfast they had simple family devotions using the *The Upper Room* booklet and Bible.

Early morning: Ken went to teach his classes early. The school was down the hill from the housing (the Mulungwishi station was set on two levels).

Early to late morning:	Lorraine home schooled the children with the Calvert Course in these early years; as a result, Kenny was able to be at home until the fourth grade. The three middle children were required to go away to boarding school at second grade, whereas Elinda attended local school through the 8th grade. When the family first arrived, Kenny attended a Swahili-speaking kindergarten.
Lunch:	Lorraine helped prepare lunch for the kindergarten and staff—down the hill. The family was generally able to eat together. Ken was not yet flying for Wings of the Morning.
Afternoon:	Lorraine taught at the women's school in the afternoon. Her courses ranged from literacy to life skills. Her days were spent running up and down the hill at the mission station—checking meal preparations, looking in on the primary school children, and teaching. Fellow missionary Woody Bartlett laughed when he told her, "I'll call you Pluto—all you do is run."

In addition to teaching at the French-speaking secondary school and administering the district Methodist churches, Ken managed the mission station farm shortly after he arrived. He was mechanically inclined and fixed many of the station's machines and building issues. "He was never afraid to work. He'd go right into the water and fix the dam if it broke; not everyone was able to do all the things he did," remembered Lorraine. She recalled a particularly interesting incident with the pigs that the station farm was raising. Evidently, they took sick from eating banana leaves. Ken got a call at 4:30 in the morning to go out and fix the piggery. Unfortunately, the entire herd had to be killed, and their carcasses burned.

Evening:

Evening meals were taken as a family in their home. Ken was sometimes away from home performing his duties as the district missionary/superintendent. Both needed evenings to prepare for the classes they were teaching. Evenings were also devoted to playing together as a growing young family.

A typical day in the bush (Sandoa):

6 a.m.:

Up at dawn for breakfast with Ken and the children. Breakfast would generally consist of oatmeal, toast, and juice if possible; oranges in season made wonderful juice. Breakfast was followed by devotions with the children. Devotions were an enduring priority; if devotions were impossible, Lorraine would gather the children in her arms and pray for God to bless and direct them that day.

Early morning to midmorning:

Lorraine home schooled the children in their early years before they went to boarding school at about second grade.

Late morning and afternoon:	Off to the women's school to "teach the teachers." She taught the basics of reading, writing, and math, as well as Bible studies and classes in childcare. Each morning she started the day checking in on the primary school, ensuring that children were in the right places at the right time. Fortunately, the director of the primary school arrived early every morning and was well able to maintain order among the classrooms. At Sandoa, Lorraine and Ken started a school for about 30 girls, building large sleeping and dining facilities for the young women.
Lunch:	Lunch was generally spent with the children; the food was simple and fresh, but took time to prepare.
Afternoon:	The children played outside during their young years at home. Most adults tried to catch a small rest in the afternoon. Lorraine would be at either of the schools, the daycare, or the dispensary in the afternoon.
Late afternoon:	Time to prepare supper. Ken normally returned home before night fell at 6 o'clock. After supper, Ken and the kids "raised a riot." They chased one another, ran around, hid in places to be discovered, played with water, and engaged in other active games. Sometimes Lorraine collapsed on the couch for a quick nap while they played.
Evening:	The family almost always had a second evening devotional. Preparation was

made for varied women's or children's groups (each was held weekly); Ken was either preparing for the next day or reading one of his beloved Louis L'Amour westerns.

Interspersed with the teaching and family responsibilities, Lorraine often organized women's conferences; went on evangelism trips with the family; or prepared for the annual camp meetings, retreats, or the Pastor's School.

Endnote

Two books were especially helpful in understanding the early work of United Methodists in Congo. They included Bishop John McKendree Springer's book, *Pioneering in the Congo*, published by New York, Katanga Press (1916) and Eva Coates Hartzler's book *Brief History of Methodist Missionary work in the Southern Congo During the First Fifty Years*, published by Methodist Church of Southern Congo, Elizabethville (1960).

The Mulungwishi mission station was founded by (future) Methodist Bishop John Springer in 1918 to be the educational center for the region. Courses in its primary school are taught in Swahili and French; beyond the primary level, all classes are taught in French. Efforts in evangelism and church planting, of which the Enrights were an integral part, have grown the Katanga Province from one Annual Conference of United Methodist Churches in 1960 (at the time of independence) to six at the present time. Membership (preparatory and full members) grew over the years from 665 in 1924; 5,292 in 1931; and 11,558 in 1945 in Congo (combined). The South Congo Conference (the southern region of the Katanga Province) grew from 20,000 in 1960 (at the time of independence), to well over 400,000 today. The North Katanga Conference (the northern region of the Katanga Province) has also seen explosive growth, with members and participants numbering about one million. North Katanga is the largest conference in the United Methodist Church today; together, these conferences in Central Africa represent the fastest growth in the denomination.

Today the Mulungwishi station includes:
- Katanga Methodist University (KMU)
- A Methodist Theological Seminary, Faculte Methodiste de Theologie (FMT)

- The Doris Bartlett Women's School (also affectionately called the Mama Doris Women's School)
- A health center (clinic and maternity care)
- Three secondary schools
- A primary school
- An agricultural project with the local community
- The United Methodist Church's Mulungwishi District headquarters.
- www.umccongo.blogspot.com: This personal blog of long-time missionaries David and Lori (daughter of Woody and Doris Bartlett) Persons chronicles life as modern missionaries. It includes much information on Mulungwishi, the work of the United Methodist Church in the region, and many of their personal experiences as lifetime missionaries at the site.
- www.youtube.com/watch?v=CAyysMgLgs0: *Mulungwishi: A United Methodist Mission* is a 27-minute video on the work at Mulungwishi. The video was awarded two 2012 Telly Awards for cinematography and religious programming.

The family thrived in their African home, adjusting well to the culture and climate of the Katanga Plateau. A fifth child, Elinda, joined siblings Kenny, John, Elaine, and Eileen several years after this photo was taken.

Ken learned farming at the Mulungwishi farm (1951).

Morning in a Lunda village as men prepare to meet with Ken and Lorraine, who had spent the night in the village. The two men seated on traditional folding chairs covered with skins were chiefs, identifiable by the skirt-like garments they wore. (Chiefs did not wear trousers.) One can also see gourds used for carrying water, women preparing food for the day (women would not be expected to participate in a meeting with important visitors), the high-end Lunda homes probably belonging to the village chief, and children. The small child in the foreground with the distended stomach was a very typical sight (early 1950s)

Cassava roots must be soaked to release their poison before being dried and pounded into flour. When mixed with water, it forms a very thick, moldable porridge and provides the foundation of the Congolese diet.

34

A woman prepares bukadi (from cassava flour) in a Congolese village. Most cooking continues to occur over charcoal fires in the outdoors (1963)

Kayeka Mutembo was a founder of the Methodist Church in Congo in the early years of the 20th century. Taken captive as a slave to Angola, he was educated in an American mission school there, later returning to Congo to help organize and teach a group of about 300 emancipated slaves and their families. Kayeka considered the first Methodist missionaries in the region an answer to his years of prayers for missionaries to come to Congo. Kayeka's memory is revered, and his influence remains in the very indigenous nature of Methodist churches in Congo. Although an old man by the time Ken and Lorraine arrived, they knew of him and worked with members of his family (photo from *Pioneering in the Congo* by John Springer)

CHAPTER 3

Sandoa, 1956-1966

"I can do all things through Christ who strengthens me."

—Philippians 4:13

In June 1955, after the family returned from their furlough in the States, they spent another year at Mulungwishi, and were then sent to their first real bush assignment in 1956. The mission station at Mwajinga was about 15 miles from a town called Sandoa Post, within a larger provincial region called Sandoa District. Sometimes, the family refers to the location of this assignment as Mwajinga, but more often as simply Sandoa. They were 650 miles from Mulungwishi, a grueling journey of at least two very long days in a carry-all, four-wheel drive vehicle they had shipped from America. Travels over Congolese roads were known as spine-pounding, neck-jarring affairs that left a person aching for days ("Worse than a horseback ride for a beginner," as Ken referred to it). Fellow missionary Woody Bartlett also gave them a pickup truck; it was old, but it ran. Unfortunately, the old truck was prone to losing a wheel occasionally, but generally it held up well to the harsh conditions. In Sandoa, Ken learned his fourth language: Lunda. Lorraine, by this time, was so busy with her teaching and work duties, raising a family, and remembering French and Swahili, that she despaired learning this new third language in such a short time and she never became fluent.

Daughter Eileen was born at the Methodist hospital at Kapanga while they were stationed at Sandoa. "Ken was supposed to be at a meeting at Lubumbashi," remembered Lorraine, "but he wouldn't leave until the baby came. As soon as Eileen was born, he left for the city, leaving a cook to help me." Ken discovered plastic on that trip to Lubumbashi and returned proudly with a brand new plastic bathtub for Eileen as well as several plastic chairs for the house.

Eileen proved to be a well-behaved but independent child. One time, Lorraine left her preschooler sleeping soundly in her bed while she and Ken made a quick trip to the church, which was very close to the house. Eileen awoke, got out of bed, found her little book bag with its Bible and songbook inside, and marched off down the road to join them. Another favorite incident took place one evening when Ken was cutting the boys' hair. Lorraine told Eileen to ask her dad for a trim while he had the clippers out. Eileen told him, "Mom wants you to cut my hair just like the boys." And so he did. Lorraine was mortified when she saw what had happened to Eileen's shock of beautiful red hair. Sometimes Ken took the kids outside to the anthills; Eileen seemed to be able to eat more ants than any of the others.

Sandoa was located in the heart of Lunda territory, about 120 miles south of Kapanga, the Lunda capital. Here, Ken and Lorraine were introduced to the Lunda people and their leadership. The Lunda were part of a kingdom that was well established and had powerful government structures in place long before the Portuguese and Belgian explorers arrived. At the top of the hierarchy was the Mwant Yav, or King. Then there were regional governors, usually identified with a large village such as Muteba. Then there were land chiefs over county-sized areas, followed by local village chiefs and villagers. This heartland was about the size of Indiana, Illinois, and Michigan. The original empire, established in the 15th century, stretched about 1,000 miles north to south and about 1,500 miles from Angola in the west, across southern Congo and ending in southeastern Zambia. During the 19th century, the Lunda traded copper, slaves, and rubber with the Portuguese on the Atlantic coast. In the 20th century, Belgium relied on the extensive Lunda leadership structure for much of the colonial administration in the tribal areas.

The Mwant Yavs encouraged the Christian missionaries, and the Enrights worked with them and other Lunda leaders to build churches, schools, and dispensaries. These leaders became personal friends and colleagues. One of the prominent African families at Sandoa was the Tschombe family. Kapend and Alphonsine Tschombe were wealthy, devout Christians who paid to build the Methodist Church at Sandoa Post. One of their sons, Moise, became president of the short-lived Katanga Republic and, later, became Congo's Prime Minister. (1) Other sons were later selected to serve in the Mwant Yav position. These leaders, as well as the common people, were sympathetic and helpful to the Christian work. The current Mwant Yav, Louis, was the youngest of the brothers and was one of Kenny's childhood friends and classmates.

Methodist missionaries first encountered the Mwant Yavs in 1910 when John Springer (who later became the first Methodist Bishop in Africa) was appointed to southern Congo. Although Catholic missionaries had been in the area for some time, the Mwant Yav especially appreciated the Methodist practice of learning the local Lunda language and sending teachers and doctors into areas needing ministry. Springer described the Mwant Yav as "a very busy, hard-working monarch" who was not only responsible for the administration of extended properties and people, but also "had to sit almost daily on native cases that were brought to him as the supreme judge." He was responsible for hundreds of workers busily building towns, for raising and supplying armed forces, for procuring food, ensuring the transportation of supplies, and for all the political and procedural administration of far-reaching governance. John Springer described the chief in his book *Pioneering in the Congo* (2) as living in a huge compound and owning large herds of cattle, pigs, sheep, and goats. He purchased his supplies (or was given them as royal tribute) of furniture, native cloth, large tents, dishes, wines, champagnes and foreign liquors, and other goods through European companies based in the Congo. He also received a percentage of royalties on rubber and other wealth, as well as taxes from his far-flung subjects. The Mwant Yav's presence was announced with calling drums, and he sat on or was carried on elaborate European seats covered with leopard or other wild animal skins. In fact, at one time all the lion and leopard skins of the country belonged to this King. A lion skin was always spread beneath his feet. His robe of state draped his figure like a Roman toga, and in addition to his elaborate, everyday headdress of bead work, he sometimes wore an immense pom-pom of scarlet feathers. While holding court, he was surrounded by royal family, also sitting on lion skins, and by court musicians playing large, fine-toned native pianos and drums.

Although the Mwant Yavs maintained close relationships with Methodist missionaries, it was not until famed British missionary to India, E. Stanley Jones, brought his Christian Ashram to Congo that one of them professed to be a Christian. Jones adapted the Hindu practice of Ashram, where people gathered in small groups under the teaching of a religious man, to a Christian context. When Jones came to southern Congo he joined Ken, Lorraine, and other missionaries in an Ashram-style camp meeting—a gathering of pastors and laity from local churches for a time of religious retreat, teaching, sharing, praying, and building community. It was the Mwant Yav in power at the time who publicly claimed his allegiance to Christ under the teaching of E. Stanley Jones. Lorraine clearly remembered the day the mighty Lunda king gave his heart to Christ.

The Mwant Yav's conversion was a momentous occasion. For many years, the Mwant Yavs had taken the message of Christianity seriously, sympathizing with the great moral message of the Bible and promoting that message without publicly embracing it themselves. The political, social, and cultural reality of such a thing seemed unthinkable. For one, Mwant Yavs were expected to have many wives (men of wealth and prestige were expected to have a large harem), and this presented a particularly difficult problem for the chief and the many women who relied on his support. (The Mwant Yav set an example for dealing with polygamy by choosing one woman to remain as his wife, while the other women in his harem remained under his care for their remaining years.) The Mwant Yav was a powerful symbol of the very essence of Lunda strength and power. The message of Jesus was that of a servant-king and was not indigenous to the Congolese. To embrace it seemed impossible. And yet, the Mwant Yav was baptized on Easter Sunday 1960, by retired Bishop John Springer, who first encountered this family of kings in 1911.

The friendships of the Lunda (including the Mwant Yavs) in South Katanga, and later the Luba tribesmen of North Katanga, were invaluable to Ken and Lorraine. Although the tribes were old enemies, they were good to the Enrights. Over the years, friends from the tribes used their influence to protect Ken and Lorraine and saved their lives in rebel uprisings. More than once, Ken was whisked away by villagers into hiding to prevent his capture by army rebels. He once told a reporter that, "The Luba tribe had vowed to take care of me," which allowed him to continue working without fear.

In Mulungwishi, the family lived about 25 miles from the larger city of Jadotville/Likasi. Although the roads were terrible and the trip a rather long hour or so, they were able to obtain food supplies in the city. In Sandoa, the family bought supplies to last for a full year. They raised a garden and kept chickens. Here the family usually hunted wild game and Lorraine became very adept at cooking varied antelope, hippopotamus, or elephant (she declared horse antelope a "most delicious meat"). Sons Kenny and John started hunting at a very young age. They received their first guns at about eight years old, followed by large ones at age 12. The boys were very comfortable on safari, conducting some on their own and hunting alone with friends when they were as young as 12. Both counted the many hunts with their father as favorite childhood memories. "I'm so glad I had my boys first," said Lorraine, "so they could learn to hunt and really enjoy the animals of the African bush." Killing an elephant or a hippo meant that everybody in the area was able to eat, generally prompting a big party and communal feast. (This chapter's endnotes describe Lorraine's favorite ways to cook large amounts of elephant or hippopotamus meat.)

Another of Lorraine's favorite memories involves an occurrence in the village of Sacundundu, a nearby village that Ken and Lorraine often visited. Sacundundu was elephant country, and the invasive elephants were notorious for stomping down and destroying local gardens. On this particular occasion, Ken had gone into the forest to kill an elephant to provide meat for everyone. Lorraine remembered that, "he had a big gun and shot the elephant, but it didn't stop the animal. The elephant came at him. Ken started to shoot again, but the gun didn't fire. He thought he would be crushed like a bug. He tried to shoot one more time; it went off and went right through the elephant's mouth and head and killed it. We sent word back to our station that if they wanted to see an elephant that had just been killed, they should come. My little daughter (second daughter, Eileen) was only 18 months old, so I took along her playpen, some mosquito netting, and all our food. The Africans were so kind to carry everything to where the elephant lay dead, waiting to be butchered and eaten. We found a lovely anthill; they cleaned off the top, set up the playpen there, and covered it with the netting."

After a prayer of thanksgiving, Ken went on to instruct the gathered crowd how to butcher the animal in an orderly fashion. Lorraine remembered being fascinated by the animal's many stomachs ("they looked like great big white pillows"). An elephant killing always meant communal meat, so women from the village carried chunks of meat in large dish pans on their heads and took them home to hungry families. It didn't take long for the entire animal to be completely divided and carried away. "What a joy that day was," she smiled. (3)

Hunts were always dangerous affairs; none more so than the Fire Hunt. One particular Fire Hunt near the village of Mwinbez (site of the roadblock incident described in Chapter four) turned tragic when one of the hunters shot another man in the abdomen. It was a sheer accident and not difficult to do considering how the village men set a ring of fire and stand at its small opening shooting the animals emerging through the fire break. The bullet tore through the man's lower abdomen and would have killed another man of lesser stock. The injured man was taken to Kafakumba, suffering massive peritonitis. Ken flew him on to the mission hospital at Matwaba, where Dr. Ray Williams performed surgery. Dr. Willliams proved himself to be a brilliant physician and surgeon; the man survived. The patient spent his days chafing at his hospitalization, requiring sedation to keep him from pulling out his IVs and spitting sugar cane all over the room.

In the meantime, the man who did the shooting was in grave danger for his life. Village protocol and local law required that he be put in jail—mostly for his own safety. The victim's family waited for revenge, believing the time would come as soon as their family member died. Indeed, local custom required that the injured man's family take some action against the shooter and his family in the event of death. Ken knew the entire situation was dangerous; he also knew the shooting was accidental and wanted to protect the shooter from harm. He asked that the shooter be brought to Lake Kafakumba instead of to jail, because it could provide a sanctuary.

It was a great day when the news came that the injured man would recover. The shooter was greatly relieved that he and his family had been spared the certain revenge of his death. He grabbed Ken's hands and bowed before him with thanksgiving. Ken then flew to Matwaba to pick up the now recovered man. When they returned to Kafakumba, Ken asked Lorraine to make tea for both men as he sat with them in the living room.

As he urged the injured man to forgive his shooter, he was surprised to hear him say, "Bwana, I've already accepted Christ as my Savior, and I have already forgiven him." The two men lived in peace; the shooter returned to his village and the recovered man continued to work at the Lake Kafakumba mission station until his recent death.

At the Sandoa mission station the family moved into a house built by a previous missionary family. Lorraine remembered that the house had a grass roof with a layer of mud over the first layer of grass. "The mud was applied so that if the roof caught fire, it wouldn't burn us all up," she said very matter-of-factly. "But the porch was not nice at all. It was still mud and had holes in it just like on a road. We tracked mud all over the house," she continued. In time, they fixed the porch and purchased linoleum squares in Lubumbashi, which Ken laid over the cement floors in the house. Yet, every house in Congo proved to be a challenge to keep clean. Not only was the presence of dirt, sand, and mud incessant, but they also had difficulty accessing water. (In Sandoa water was hauled from the river to fill large tanks that then provided gravity-fed water to the house. In Mulungwishi, the water was hauled in barrels up the mission station's long hill. Always their water had to settle and then be boiled for drinking.)

The house in Sandoa had no indoor plumbing when the family arrived, and the bathroom was just outside of the house—close enough to their bedroom that they didn't actually have to go outside to use it. Fortunately, Ken was a handyman, and it wasn't long before he ran water lines and built an indoor bathroom with running water. Lorraine was thrilled to take a bath in warm water, and more so to bathe the children in the warm water. She recalled once leaving a local woman in charge of her very small children and hearing them screaming and carrying on from the cold water bath they were being given. Lorraine decided then and there that she and Ken would arrange childcare duties so that one of them would always be with the young children—and they would be given warm baths and other care she found more to her liking.

The home had a separate building for a kitchen, complete with a wood stove. Later, Lorraine obtained a gas stove, but it was reserved for foods that required a short cooking time; generally they used the wood stove to prepare food. Fruits and vegetables grew in abundance, and the family by necessity ate very simply. Daughter Elinda (now a registered nurse) continues to believe that their family's good health and her mother's continued vitality into old age can be attributed to the simple, but nutritious and natural foods they ate in Africa.

Because Sandoa was in the bush, the family enjoyed seeing wildlife all around them. Horse antelope (a favorite meat for eating) were plentiful and gathered in large grazing herds of 100 or more in the fields around them. They also had many monkeys, even keeping one as a pet. "The kids just loved it," remembered Lorraine. She was thankful later when that same monkey was out with daughter Elaine and climbed up a tree, chattering relentlessly from a protruding limb. When Elaine looked up, she saw a huge snake right over her head and quickly got out of harm's way. Considering the potency of the area's poisonous snakes, the family figures that the monkey saved her life.

In Sandoa, Ken was responsible for all the churches in both the Sandoa and Kafakumba districts. This meant he was out preaching in different churches every Sunday, holding district retreats and training sessions, and eventually developing a curriculum for a multi-week pastors' school. He also managed building new churches throughout the district or at least providing technical help and overseeing others in their building. Former missionaries Bill and Doris Davis started work in the district but were moved to the Kapanga Mission Station before churches were built to house new congregations in the area. Ken became a master at overseeing the construction of church buildings. He recruited and employed men from the villages to build their churches, creating buildings that were totally African and fit naturally into their surroundings. Many times he flew out to remote villages, staying up all night to ensure the kilns remained heated for brickmaking and ensure that construction progressed as scheduled. Across Southern Congo, hundreds of these simple structures were built with homemade clay bricks from local soils and topped with wood trusses and tin roofs. Making and stacking the bricks was hard work, but accomplished rather easily by local villagers. The wood trusses and tin roofs were too expensive for local congregations to purchase, so Ken set himself to raising funds to build roofs for churches. And, the task of getting supplies to remote villages inaccessible by roads or rivers was a constant challenge. Sadly, some of the churches were later destroyed by invading rebels in Congo's long conflicts, and their tin roofs stolen for money. The challenge remains in Congo today to roof the walls of old and new churches; sometimes Lorraine still sends money for a roof here or there.

Lorraine was responsible for the primary school at Sandoa. So many children wanted to go to school that they had to set age limits for the students. They thus devised this standard: any young man in third grade or below who had hair under his arms was too old for the primary school and must be dismissed. This left more room for younger children. Lorraine remembered the children as being happy bunches of smiling faces, who loved playing games and doing their schoolwork.

Lorraine's favorite work at Sandoa, however, was working with adolescent girls; she and Ken started a boarding school for girls there. Lorraine began to work with the girls as they grew into adolescence (at about 11 years old), helping them with their studies, and teaching them how to sew and cook and keep a healthy home. About 21 girls up to 16 years old stayed right on the mission stations at both Mulungwishi and Sandoa. "We put a wonderful Christian woman in charge," she said, "and we worked together all the time. I had so much fun working with the girls at Sandoa, just so much fun." As at Mulungwishi, she experienced the transformation of the school's leadership and teachers from the white missionaries in earlier years to a totally indigenous Congolese leadership.

It was also at Sandoa that Lorraine began working more intentionally with women. She organized and led women's conferences that lasted three or four days. Ken cared for their children while she worked with the women, but he always came at the women's request to speak on their last night together. "It was at Sandoa that we decided that all the African and missionary women would sleep together in the same place. We made a circle of grass about 1½ to 2 feet tall to enclose us. Then, we put grass on the ground to sleep on. It was a joy to sing together and pray together. The African women knew we didn't always eat their food, and they prepared special food for us that we were happy to eat. Many of the ladies accepted Christ and had a real desire to follow Jesus. Many came to the Lord when my husband held the closing service." For Lorraine, the women's meetings were a time of great joy and some of her favorite memories of their decades of ministry. After one of the conferences, a district superintendent, Paul Mbang, said to her, "Mama, I want you to know this was the most wonderful meeting we have had, because you missionary ladies were able to come and stay in the same house with our African Christian ladies. I want to thank you."

From a Sandoa letter:

Dear Friends in Christ:

This summer was a time of fulfillment...a summer beyond explanation, but one that will be relived many times in the future. The statistics cannot explain it, but they are a necessary part of it....Over 1,000 decisions for Christ...over fifty lives saved in emergencies....43 students in the Bible courses for pastors.... and a Super Wedding with eleven couples getting married. And, if that isn't enough, I'll sprinkle in a building program of two churches, two houses, and a dispensary, along with three bad accidents and an eleven-ton truck driven in the Lake.

Figures only blur a picture in my mind, for I think of Kayembe in terms of one of the most beautiful conversions I have ever seen. The Chief's decision drew more attention and was more dramatic. And the hundreds coming to the altar is certainly an impressive sight....But let me tell you about the conversion that meant so much to me.

One wonderful Christian worker, Marie Nakalenda, who has been instrumental in founding three churches, is an old lady. One night she went to another old lady, who had been her friend for years and years. She said, "We have walked through life together for many years. Let's both walk together in the future. Will you give up your witchcraft and accept Christ? IN THE MORNING THIS OLD LADY WHO WAS BENT ALMOST DOUBLE WITH AGE AROSE AND BROUGHT HER CALABAS OF MEDICINES AND IDOLS TO THE ALTAR. When I saw her shrunken and infirmed body I thought, it is a good thing this meeting wasn't delayed for she doesn't have many days left. As the two old ladies left the church to go home to their huts they walked hand in hand. Someday they will walk hand in hand with Christ to another home and they too will thank God for this wonderful summer.

The fifty lives saved is a conservative figure, for I am only thinking of the emergencies and not the crowds that our little dispensary has treated each day....One emergency was a man who couldn't walk and who had lost the sense of feeling in his legs and hips. (It turned out to be a tumor on the spine.) I flew him to Kapanga, and the doctor started preliminary examinations. While this was being done, I talked with him about accepting Christ. I said, "Look, you feel bad and bitter because you can't use your legs. Look around and you will see friends and people who can't use their heads... They are drunk and rotting and going from one sin to a worse mess. You can use your head; think and seek the Lord. You have eyes—look. You've got a heart—pray." After a *half hour he accepted Christ. I don't know if he will ever get rid of that tumor, but I do know he got rid of a lot of other problems and grief.*

I'm running out of space so I'll just say that I was teaching about marriage and a Christian home. I stressed the need of seeking the blessing of God on marriage.

> *Yours in Christ,*
> *Ken and Lorraine Enright*

Because Ken and Lorraine were also assigned to the adjoining Kafakumba District, as well as Sandoa, Ken found himself stretched by the preaching and evangelistic services he held in outlying areas. He had also been starting schools and health dispensaries, raising funds for tin roofs, and flying. It was during their years at Sandoa that they began using a boat for revival services. They dubbed the boat *The African Queen* and located it at Luena. Here, they would load it up with their family and supplies and set off to reach villages deep in a valley along the Lualaba River that were not accessible by roads. At Sandoa, they also purchased a small, pull-behind camper for their family when they headed out to villages for week-long evangelistic services.

The purchase and transport of the camper was a favorite memory for Lorraine. She remembered picking it up in Zambia at the same time they were picking up new missionaries, Dr. Glenn and Lena Eschtruth and family. "Everybody wanted to travel with Ken because he could always get through roadblocks without much hassle" she remembered. Furthermore, Ken's people skills with uncooperative, sometimes angry and drunken soldiers at roadblocks became legendary. He also knew the best routes in and out of the country. This time, he chose to bring the Eschtruths through Angola, into Zambia, and then planned to make the border crossing into Congo at Muchacha.

He and Lorraine had just purchased the camper in Zambia and the two family groups arrived at the border crossing. Soldiers demanded that Ken tell them what they were bringing with them. The soldiers badgered the family many times with their questions, "What did you bring? What are bringing into the country?" They searched the cars and their contents but could never figure out what the families had brought. "What did we bring? Why we brought the house trailer," laughed Lorraine with the biggest laugh possible, "but they didn't even know it! We got the Eschtruths to their station at Kapanga, so they were happy. We took the trailer to villages when we had meetings, and we were happy," she continued. The camper came in mighty handy on rainy and cool days, especially when holding revivals during the rainy season. Lorraine remembered using pans of warm water to wash the children's feet, cooking meals on the camper's little gas stove, and sleeping tight in its one double bed and two children each in its two single beds. The camper also provided extra space for guests when parked beside the house at Lake Kafakumba.

Again, Ken became known for being a prodigious worker. He immersed himself fully into Luba culture and was embraced wholly by those with whom he worked. He loved the people surrounding him, especially those in the area's many villages. He was a man driven—by his own experiences, his passion and personality, and the enormity of the work. He understood the meaning of his calling and threw himself fully into sharing the teachings of Christ.

"I was having so much fun, such fun, teaching the young ladies at Sandoa," remembered Lorraine, "and then the war came and upset the fruit basket." *Upset the fruit basket.* That's probably the most benign description of the horrific wars, upheaval, and anguish following Congo's independence from Belgian rule that was ever uttered. War came, the school children were sent back to their villages, and the Enright family returned to the United States for their second furlough. It was 1960. The other Methodist mission families were evacuated from the country, and the Congolese sought shelter from marauding militias any way they could. Ken and Lorraine remained far from the struggle at Embry Riddle Aeronautical

University in Florida; it was during this furlough that Ken met airplanes. (See Chapter 10, "Flying," for a brief glimpse into the Wings of the Morning flying ministry and the passion with which Ken embraced flight.)

Ken and Lorraine returned to Sandoa and Kafakumba in 1961. Although the war had devastated much of the region, they found their homes at both places intact, thanks to their African friends protecting the areas. The effects of war were immediately evident. "We couldn't get our mail any longer," lamented Lorraine. Letters were lifelines for the family during their years in Congo and meant everything to them. "Under Belgian rule, I could at least order from the Sears catalog," Lorraine remembered, "but after independence we could not do that." With fabric unavailable in Congo and the clothing needs of a growing family always changing, Lorraine sorely missed that resource. In fact, many of the missionaries missed ordering from the Sears catalog. It was the custom for mission moms to check out the new catalog at the beginning of the year and order their children's clothing for the following year. The orders would arrive just in time for Annual Conference, at which time the missionary families arrived with children dressed alike as if it were planned that way. Lorraine's friend and sister-in-law, Dorothy Farrier (Chester's wife), would send frilly dresses for the Enright girls every spring, and up-to-date, fashionable clothing for Lorraine. That welcome luxury stopped in 1960 as well. Roads, schools, hospitals, governance, and local services were all pretty much destroyed in the ensuing years of upheaval and violence.

The missionary community experienced the horrors of Congo's post-independence years in full. The country was ill-prepared for self-rule, with Belgians having held the positions of power in government, business, and the military. Very few Congolese had the education or experience needed to fill the sizeable vacuum left when Belgium departed. Political alliances emerged (often based on ethnicity and allegiance to a particular region of the country), which struggled violently for power and control of the new country.

Another contributing factor to the region's instability was the location of Congo in the African struggle between Communism and Democracy, with the West and its Communist enemies taking aim at each other straight through the hearts of the Congolese. Angola, with its Cuban advisors and international mercenaries, welcomed both renegade and rebel soldiers from Congo. Over the years many militia forces moved back and forth across Katanga between Congo and Angola, making the province a dangerous place to live.

In addition, Northern Rhodesia (which bordered Congo on its southern flank and is now named Zambia) was fighting its own war of independence and became a target for violence, political upheaval, and East-West tensions. Finally, Katanga's incredible mineral wealth made it a target for control by just about everyone involved. So, in this complex context of competing powers without and within, constant upheaval remained, including violent rebel alliances and activities and danger for all who lived in the region. The on-line *Encyclopedia Britannica* described the situation this way: "After gaining complete independence from Belgium in 1960, a non-stop parade of assassinations, civil wars, coups, corrupt dictators, brutal murders, rebellions and needless bloodshed plagued the land." The Congo that Ken and Lorraine returned to in 1961 had, indeed, changed forever.

But the certainty of their call to be in ministry with the people of Congo never faltered. "When you know you're called by the Lord, you just do it," said Lorraine. After a thoughtful pause, a short time perhaps filled with memories of both hardship and joy, she added softly, "We never shirked."

Although life became much more difficult after independence, Ken and Lorraine continued serving at both Sandoa and Kafakumba for six more years after returning from their second furlough. They maintained homes in each place, because they were assigned to work with churches in both districts. Many Christians lived in the Kafakumba area, and 12 churches had been built, with still more to be done. By this time, Ken had also added flying to his list of things to do—meaning that in addition to preaching, teaching, holding Pastor's School, planting and building churches, building schools and dispensaries, and raising money for their many projects, he also became a missionary pilot. This meant overseeing the building of air strips in remote villages and mission sites around the region, flying patients to hospitals or flying mission personnel between sites, as well as doing mechanical work on the planes.

Airplanes made life much easier for the missionaries. The eight hour drive from Sandoa to Kafakumba was reduced to 20 minutes by air. Food and supplies could be purchased on one of Ken's scheduled trips to a city, rather than planning food supplies for an entire year. "He kept a little spot under the right, front seat for things I ordered," smiled Lorraine. Even more important, he evacuated missionaries many times when mission sites were threatened by invading armies. He founded the Methodist flight ministry, Wings of the Morning, with fellow-pilot Paul Alexander. The ministry grew to include several pilot/missionaries and continues to serve the Katanga Conferences today. All of its pilots are now Congolese who grew up on Methodist mission stations and were trained by missionaries in the field.

Sandoa endnote:

(1)   Moise Tshombe received his education at a Methodist Mission School and had long been involved with the Methodist church in southern Congo. Missionaries in Katanga knew him well. After Congo's independence in 1960, he led the rebellion of the southern, mineral-rich province of Katanga against the new, centralized government, creating an independent state sympathetic to Belgian and other Western interests. To maintain a unified country, Katanga's army was defeated after the United Nations intervened and Katanga rejoined the United Republic of Congo. Tshombe went on to serve for a short time as the country's prime minister, helping to quell a rebellion by eastern provinces. He was kidnapped in 1967 and taken to Algeria, where he was held under house arrest until his death in 1969 (Source: *Encyclopedia Britannica*)

Moise Tshombe's picture was on the front cover of *Time* Magazine on December 22, 1961, highlighting its key article "Struggle for the Congo."

(2)   Information about the Mwant Yav kings was taken from Bishop John McKendree Springer's book, *Pioneering in the Congo*, published by New York, Katanga Press, in 1916.

(3)   Lorraine insisted that her recipe for cooking large amounts of elephant or hippopotamus produced the moistest, most delicious meat ever. She used it many times in preparing wild game for large groups at camp meetings or during Pastors' School. Perhaps the technique remains transferable to other meat in other situations.

Wild Game Recipe

In Lorraine's own words: "One of the Africans taught us how to cook a hippo in a way that resulted in the most delicious meat ever. First, you dig a deep hole in the ground. Place wood of every description into this great big hole. After the fire is burning brightly and you know it is hot (this may take a day or an evening), place large stones into the hole and keep throwing on more fire until the stones are red hot. Wash 20 gunny sacks so they are nice and clean. Cut up the hippo into large pieces, put salt on it and place the pieces in the bags. Place the bags of meat on top of the stones and cover with a large canvas tarp, which you then cover with sand and dirt so no air can get down into the meat. Allow it to cook overnight. At about 2:00 or 3:00 the next afternoon you will have the most beautiful, tasty meat in the whole world. And there is so much of it! It would serve a lot of people, and we shared it with all the Africans in our school. You can cook an elephant the same way only longer and in a bigger hole. Putting it in the clean bags worked very nicely. If you got a young elephant the meat was delicious; if it was an older one the meat was tough, so I made it into hamburger."

The killing of an elephant was an event for the entire village, providing meat for everyone in the area. After Ken shot this elephant, Lorraine brought the children to observe the festivities. Wild game and fish provided meat for the attendees at Pastors' School in Congo for many years.

Ken hunting in the Kafakumba District in the 1960s. Ken's hunting skills brought him status and respect among the Africans of the Katanga Province.

Children John, Elaine, and Eileen gathered with their parents for the daily routine of family devotions.

Lorraine with John and Elaine at the Sandoa mission station (1957).

Village chiefs are powerful ethnic and political leaders, providing an important layer of governance at the local level.

The wooden mortar and pestle remain at the center of food preparation. Greens of every sort are pounded (pumpkin leaves and rapeseed are popular), as are corn and cassava. Cooking is simple, but very hard work.

Women provide the heavy labor for clearing fields. With very primitive tools they can be seen working in fields all day, often with a baby on their back.

Ken and Lorraine communicated regularly with their families and supporters back in the States. The old camper seen here was taken to camp meetings and revivals as a home for the family in the villages. It ended its life as overflow housing at Lake Kafakumba.

During a furlough from Sandoa, Ken learned of the need for pilots and airplanes to support Methodist missions in Congo. He returned to Africa with a pilot's license and started the Wings of the Morning ministry with fellow missionary pilot, Paul Alexander. The men became lifesavers for staff and patients at Kapanga Methodist Hospital (now Samuteb Memorial Hospital) in southwest Congo.

CHAPTER 4

Lake Kafakumba, 1961–1998

"He has shown you, O man, what is good. And what does the Lord require of you? To act justly and to love mercy and to walk humbly with your God."
—Micah 6:8

Lake Kafakumba—Place of ministry

Ken and Lorraine found themselves gradually spending more and more of their time in the Kafakumba District. Several missionaries were already living and working at the Sandoa site, so Ken found himself gravitating toward this second district to which he was assigned. Fellow missionary and pilot Bill Davis had been preaching very successfully in the area, but had been moved to another mission station. Now Ken found scattered congregations growing quickly and his own preaching so fruitful that many churches were springing up in the region—so many that it was difficult to find pastors for all of them.

An incident that occurred on a road one night illustrates this desperate need for pastors. Ken and Lorraine were driving with their family near the village of Mwinbez (1) when they encountered a road block. Road blocks were common—tense, unpredictable encounters with soldiers—and unnerving. This time, however, it wasn't soldiers blocking the road, but men from Mwinbez. Ken recognized the villagers and asked if there was a problem. Well, yes, there was, they responded. Ken had promised to get them a pastor for three years, and they had done their part by building their church. They now wanted their promised pastor. Their patience had run out, and they resorted to the roadblock to force the issue. The men of the village produced a paper and pen and someone who could write up a simple agreement. They then extracted a written promise from Ken to produce a pastor before they would allow the family to use "their road." Village leaders were very serious about their need and finally took the matter into their own hands. Before long, they had a pastor. The people of this village remained very loyal to the Enrights through all their years in Congo.

"Sometimes one gets the idea that the Congolese were just poor, helpless victims," recalled son Kenny. "That was far from true. They were aggressive, and there was tremendous local interest in church and faith. We were constantly bombarded by people wanting my father's help in getting their churches built. Or, they'd tell him that they were ready for a school and ask what should be done about it." Kenny always believed that his father's unusual status and prestige with the Africans had everything to do with his principles and courage; that and the fact that, "he was very good at what he did." Kenny laughed as he continued, "My father was really a subversive Irishman who would always back the poor against the elites any day of the week. And, he would show it."

It became clear to Ken that the need for training village pastors was urgent. But many had limited schooling and would never be candidates for training at the Methodist University or Seminary at Mulungwishi, which were more academically and theoretically oriented. Ken wanted very practical training for village pastors—to teach them what they needed to preach, how to counsel and lead Bible study, how to promote public health and good moral considerations. In Congo, it seemed, everyone was desperate to learn to do their job correctly. Rural pastors served in isolated places scattered throughout the area, separated by distance and difficult travel. Although the missionaries and district superintendents worked constantly to support the need for pastors, the job became overwhelming in its piecemeal approach.

So the idea was planted for some kind of organized, goal-oriented pastoral training, the practical kind that rode well on the hard seat of a bicycle. Ken knew just the person to ask to help him make it happen—Marv Wolford—and where to hold it—Lake Kafakumba. Marv began his career as a short-term Methodist mission intern to Congo who returned to the country and became a lifelong friend and colleague in ministry with Ken. Lake Kafakumba had been the site of several successful camp meetings and provided an ideal location for a pastor gathering. They would call this new endeavor Kafakumba Pastors' School.

Village pastors became the passion of Ken's life. Pastoring, both being a pastor and nurturing other pastors, was his primary ministerial focus. During his early years, he was mentored by the finest among Congolese pastors. They helped him understand their culture, bridged the greatest of divides between American and African sensibilities, advised him, respected him, patiently befriended him, sometimes protected him, hunted with him, shared their homes and tables with him, and inspired his faith. These were honorable men, leaders among their people, and in the Methodist churches in Congo, men who loved God and had committed their lives in difficult circumstances to serving Him. Men like Silas Mwamba, Jason Sendwe, Joab Mulela, Matwafadi Morrison, John Kalesa, Paul Kapenbamoto, Joel Bulaya, Paul Mbang, Moise Ndua, and Albert Makumbi shared their lives and influence with Ken. He loved them in return and devoted his life to lifting them up.

Whether speaking, flying, training others, preaching and evangelizing, building churches and airstrips, founding ministries of mercy such as feeding programs or providing medical care—all were done within the framework of pastoral ministry. "He was a pastor first. That is always where his heart was," confirmed daughter Elinda. She remembered the many times he flew to remote places, even building airstrips to get there, so that he could work with a local pastor in a little village. "He was truly a pastor of pastors," she added. The influence of these African pastors and leaders was incalculable as the shape of Kafakumba Pastors' School began to emerge.

Lorraine remembered their first trip to Lake Kafakumba, where they and the Wolfords were going to hold a camp meeting. They arrived late at night. The lake was so far removed in the bush, and it was so dark, that Marv finally asked Ken where in the world they were. Ken laughed and told him that if he drove any farther he'd be in the lake. Sure enough, they arrived on the shores of Lake Kafakumba. "It was one of the most beautiful places in the world," remembered Lorraine with a sigh. There were no buildings on the site, and the families slept in their cars that night. It didn't take long, though, to settle in. Over the next few days, little grass huts were built and space was staked out for a mud brick home for the Enright family. The early camp meetings and those early sessions of pastors' school were simple affairs held on the lakeshore. While Ken and Marv taught pastors, Lorraine and Jean stayed busy teaching the wives and children, as well as caring for their own children and cooking.

And so the school began in 1963.

Kafakumba Pastors' School

"Five men on a log" was how Ken described those early days of Pastors' School in a letter to supporters. He participated in starting the Methodist Seminary at Mulungwishi and had seen many pastors receive seminary training for their lives as Methodist ministers and administrators. Over time, he observed that almost all of the seminary's graduates entered leadership positions in the Congolese church—as bishops, superintendents, administrators, or pastors of the largest churches. He became concerned that the local village pastors took on responsibilities and leadership for which they received no training. He believed that these pastors were the heart of the church in Africa and grew to love and care for them with extraordinary passion. Their preparation and well-being as pastors of the emerging village churches became the focus of his ministry for the rest of his life. Kafakumba Pastors' School held its first classes in 1963 and continued to do so through wars, political upheaval, destruction, and relocation across Congo's southern border to Zambia.

In its earliest days, the Pastors' School had no classrooms, tables, chairs, or teaching devices. As aural learners and story-tellers, however, the pastors were eager students. They brought much of what they needed with them, including simple food supplies such as palm oil, vegetables, and manioc flour, and turned to the lake for fish. The Enright sons, Kenny and John, became excellent hunters and with other African hunters pro-vided mostly antelope meat for the pastors and others at the school. Hunting to provide meat for Pastors' School, or any large gathering, was serious business. Local people relied heavily on hunting for meat, because cattle did not fare well in the tsetse fly infested area. Both Kenny and John became excellent marks-men, taking down every size of wild animal and earning the respect of those who hunted with them.

Because wives and children came with the men, Lorraine and Jean Wolford soon found themselves holding classes for the women and children. For 20 years, the Kafakumba Pastors' School consisted of courses taught over two to four week peri-ods, with the entire curriculum completed in four to five years. Pastors' School took place after the rainy season, generally in April or May, when roads became passable.

In 1984, when the Pastors' School had existed for 20 years, John Enright took over leadership of the school. A Methodist missionary in his own right, John was seminary trained and was first assigned to teach in Botswana and then went on to church planting, education, and administration in Congo. John restruc-tured the curriculum into one modeled after Asbury Seminary, his father's alma mater. He determined the hours needed for a seminary degree at Asbury and applied them to the curriculum at Kafakumba, thus stretching the program from two weeks to six weeks and from four years to eight years. Classes became more structured and included topics such as Church History, Inductive Bible Study, Old Testament and New Testament Surveys, and Homiletics (Preaching). The number of instructors increased and began to include theologically trained missionaries from the region, as well as Congolese teachers. Ken Vance, Methodist missionary in Congo and Zambia, has taught at the school for many years and continues to live and work at the Kafakumba campus in Zambia. Marv Wolford taught at Kafakumba all his years in Congo, especially enjoying his topic of the "Christian Response to Witchcraft"—the theme of his doctoral dissertation and a topic very useful to African pastors. Marv later spent many years translating the Bible into the Lunda language.

Although the Pastors' School was rooted in an African application of theological training, it was not uncommon for pastors and teachers from the United States and other countries to travel to Congo—and later Zambia—to teach parts of a section or two in the school. Some provided two to four weeks of teaching every year for many years; others participated only occasionally. But for all those who taught or participated in the Pastors' School in some way, all considered it a highlight of their year, even of their lives.

As the school grew, more buildings were built at Lake Kafakumba. The little grass huts were replaced by small mud brick homes, where the pastors and their families lived while at school. Although pastors attended the first four years alone, they were allowed to bring wives and families for their last four years of classes. Classes for wives and children developed under the direction of Lorraine and Jean Wolford; indeed, over the years a variety of classes, taught by varied missionaries or African teachers, greatly enriched the lives of the wives and families. When asked about the School's impact on their lives, very often the pastors replied that it was the effect of the program on their wives that made the biggest difference in their lives. Certainly these women had a huge impact not only on their churches, but also on the daily lives of those in the villages around them. For children, the daily lessons and activities meant that they enjoyed a great adventure in learning and loving at Lake Kafakumba. Their experiences stood in marked contrast to the often dismal lives of other children back home in their respective villages.

Part of Kafakumba's design was to keep clergy in their villages for the duration of their schooling. This was unlike the situation for those who left their homes for an education in a city or even at Mulungwishi Methodist University. Those students rarely returned to village life, but stayed in the cities for work or were assigned to senior church administrative roles. Kafakumba clergy, however, left home for only eight weeks each year and returned to their home and pastorate until the next year. Because their curriculum focused on very practical applications of their pastoral training, the intervening ten months proved to be an excellent laboratory for new understandings. Pastors were given time to assimilate what they had learned, to try new things in their communities, and to recognize and form the questions that came back with them the following year. It has proven to be an effective pattern of teaching and remains integral to the Kafakumba model today.

Endnote

1. Mwinbez was an unusual village in West Katanga. It was known for its strong communal spirit and the villagers' unusual practice of raising a community garden in which everyone participated. The garden resulted from a vote taken by the villagers. The church remains strong and growing in the village.

"The most beautiful place in the world" was how Lorraine described Congo's Lake Kafakumba. The lake teemed with fish and was surrounded by an unusual tropical forest.

Their home at Lake Kafakumba was a simple, sun-dried brick structure with no plumbing or electricity for many years (note the clear corrugated fiberglass that provided plentiful interior light). The family lived here part-time every year from 1964 until 1998, when Ken and Lorraine evacuated for the last time. Lake Kafakumba became a beloved home for the family, as well as an important mission site. The schools, hospital, and church remain strong.

Lorraine's daycare at Lake Kafakumba served lunch daily to many children. A typical lunch of bukadi (made from the flour of cassava roots), greens, and dried fish was often the children's only meal of the day.

Ken started and oversaw the building of the church at Lake Kafakumba. The church was part of a larger campus that included an elementary school, classrooms, and living quarters for those attending Kafakumba Pastors' School each year, a medical dispensary and small hospital, a daycare, houses for teachers, homes for missionaries, and a runway and hangar for the Wings of the Morning airplane Ken flew.

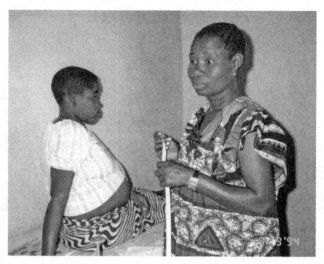

The "dispensaire Methodiste" (medical dispensary) was an important part of Methodist mission stations, and Lorraine's early interest in nursing was put to good work. The clinic at Kafakumba provided primary care, including a busy maternity ward staffed by midwives. A small hospital with an attending physician and nurses provided most care; emergencies were flown to larger facilities. Pictured here, a midwife checks and measures a mother-to-be.

New graduates of the part-time, eight-year program to become local pastors celebrated their graduation with gifts of matching jackets. They were one of the last classes to graduate at the Lake Kafakumba site, as war made it impossible to continue operating the school in the region.

Including the pastors' wives and families was always an important part of Kafakumba Pastors' School. Many pastors considered their wives experience at the school the most important part of their training. As part of the program for four of their husband's eight years, these women celebrated their own graduations.

Something was always going on with the kids during the Pastors' School at Lake Kafakumba.

71

Teachers, nurses, wives, church leaders...something was always going on for women at Lake Kafakumba.

Lake Kafakumba: A place called home, 1962–1998

Lake Kafakumba became a second, and much loved, home for the Enrights from the time Ken was assigned to the Kafakumba District along with his duties at Sandoa in the late 1950s. "It was beautiful, just so-o-o beautiful," remembered Lorraine. Her children all echoed her sentiment as they recounted the beautiful water, with its plentiful store of fish; the unusual trees and wild animals of the surrounding forest; the richness of the soil; and prolific fruit such as strawberries, papaya "the size of melons," pineapple, and the ever-present bananas. Plentiful fruits and vegetables were available year-round.

Lake Kafakumba was also a "very strange place," remembered son, John. Located at the headwaters of the Sankuru Lueo River, a tropical rainforest developed around it, even though it was surrounded by savannahs further out. The area was part of a huge swamp, filled with cypress groves growing out into the lake. Monkeys filled the trees and wild game was plentiful in the surrounding woods, swamps, and grasslands. Legends of mythical creatures filling the lake were common. Villagers, however, had moved away from the water's edge, probably because of malaria, so its shores were completely empty when the Enrights and Wolfords had arrived that night with plans for upcoming camp meetings.

The site was central to the many growing Methodist congregations in the area and became a favored spot for extended church camp meetings and retreats. Ken had decided to build a small, mud brick house on the shore to house his family when they were there. Its construction took some time because mud bricks took time to dry in the sun. If they weren't fired, or didn't dry long enough, they would slump from the rain and weather and tumble down. Eventually the tiny lake house was completed with sun-dried brick, and it became a family home for the remainder of their years in Congo. One could sometimes hear shrews scurrying about the home's open rafters. It was several years before the house had running water and indoor plumbing. "When I became pregnant with Elinda, we finally got an indoor toilet at Kafakumba, so I felt like we had the situation well in hand," remembered Lorraine. Oldest son Kenny never remembered such amenities and took all of his baths in the lake. An outdoor gravity-fed tank that was fired with wood from below was the only way they ever had hot water at the house.

Living just 30 or 40 feet from the water's edge, the lake became an integral part of their lives. Not only did the family and others enjoy the water for recreation, but more importantly it supplied plentiful fish. "We loved the fish from that lake," recalled Lorraine, "especially the tilapia." Lorraine fried the fish in pancake batter, declaring it the tastiest fish they'd ever eaten. The lake provided a living for local fisherman and all the fish needed for the mission station's needs.

The Lake Kafakumba site proved to be a good location for a variety of ministries and grew far beyond its use for camp meetings and Pastors' School. Although there had already been buildings at other mission sites, there was nothing but bush at Kafakumba. Ken and Lorraine envisioned the ministries together, and then Ken oversaw the construction of all of the buildings at the site—primary and secondary schools, churches (in surrounding villages and at the lake), a dispensary, daycare, training center, classrooms, a shelter for extra children's classes, residences for teachers, and residences for the families of patients in the dispensary. He built an airstrip along the water's edge, a hangar for the airplane, a fruit orchard and garden, even a nine-hole golf course. The golf course provided recreation for Ken and other Africans who took up golf and played with him. They teed off from leveled anthills, drove balls down the landing strip-turned-fairway, and putted into holes surrounded by sand smoothed by the players of each game. Dubbed the Kafakumba Country Club, the course was a testament to Ken's playful ingenuity and creativity. All of the buildings at the site were built well, even the unfired brick ones, and remain standing today. Education, healthcare, and feeding are still being provided. The church is strong. The mission station remains fully operational, with all of its ministries thriving and all of its administration provided by Congolese leadership. "This was really my father's dream," said John. "He created everything there."

For the Enright family, though, Lake Kafakumba was simply home. Although they had a primary home in each of the stations to which they were assigned after the late 1950s (Sandoa, Kolwezi, Lubumbashi, Manono), they also had co-assignments to Kafakumba, and the lake was central to the work they did in that district. It was the place to which the children returned from their varied boarding schools during school vacations. It was the home at which many visitors, friends, and missionaries shared a meal at their table. It became a campus filled with many ministries, a bustle of people, and a center for the growing network of Methodist churches in southern Congo. "There were a lot of Christians in the Kafakumba area," said Lorraine, "and the people were always just so good to us." It continues to hold a very special place in the heart of each family member.

The lake was large—about a mile wide and five miles long. For the adult Enright children, favorite memories of the lake always include fishing. All three girls, now grown and separated by years from life at Kafakumba, remember fishing as their favorite activity at the lake. Elinda, because she did not go to boarding school until 9th grade, enjoyed the most time at Lake Kafakumba. She and a couple little friends spent many days catching and drying small fish that they in turn sold at market. "We'd be on the water by about six in the morning and fish until noon. After lunch, we'd fish again until about six," she said. The three-some dried the fish on sticks, layering them in the bright sun, and then sent them off to a distributor in the city with Ken when he flew out. Fishing alone, with their father, with each other, with friends, from a canoe, on the shore, for large fish or small—all of the Enright children loved fishing.

Lorraine laughed as she remembered initiating family members and others into Kafakumba-ites. "The children had to walk a gauntlet of fallen trees. When they could do it without falling off, we christened them Kafakumba-ites." Ken made protecting the surrounding old-growth tropical forest a priority and forbade anyone from cutting trees beyond a certain point to protect the habitat. The water, of course, created a beautiful vista that everyone enjoyed. Lorraine filled a dilapidated canoe with flowers and placed it at the water's edge. Ken built a dock and enclosed a swimming area to help protect swimmers from stray crocodiles.

Along with the shoreline view, however, came a host of poisonous and dangerous wildlife: snakes of varied sorts and the crocs made their home at the water's edge, too. Ken worked for years to kill crocodiles, only somewhat successfully, but never eliminated danger from their surroundings. It didn't hamper the family's enthusiasm, though, and they spent many hours boating, water skiing, swimming, and diving in the warm waters. Once they even fashioned a homemade wooden slalom ski that worked perfectly well until they purchased a manufactured ski.

Lorraine captured some typical moments at the lake in a letter to son Kenny, who by then was living in the U.S.:

Lake Kafakumba

"Well, your littlest sister has just inherited the Honda Hunter (a small motorcycle). Elinda does a fine job riding it and giving rides to her friends on the airstrip. The girls both do a good job of keeping up on water skis. Eileen is learning to slalom now. They and the crocs are doing great. We do hope to get the crocs killed, but you know how hard they are to get. Well, Dad is calling us to go to church and the car is up here now."

Living at Lake Kafakumba was not always a bed of roses. It, too, was caught in political intrigue and fighting during the years in which Mobutu Sese Seko was president. During those many years, rebellions occurred across Katanga at will, as one group after another fought to wrest power from an entrenched, corrupt government. During the 1980s President Mobutu could not pay his military and passively allowed them to pillage businesses and ordinary people's residences as their compensation. This was known as Le Pillage, and it created a distinct era of chaos. Although the country received billions of dollars in aid and owned vast expanses of mineral wealth, very little money made its way to Congo's common people. Roadblocks, violent raids on villages, thefts of private homes and goods, pillage by customs at the borders—all were carried out with impunity against its country's citizens.

One particular incident of Le Pillage highlighted the danger in the region. Ken had received word that the Army was moving toward Ngongo (the main village a mile from Lake Kafakumba) from the neighboring area near Kasaji. The men of the village asked Ken what they should do. They told him that if he would stay and lead them, they would stand and fight. But if he left, they would go into hiding in the bush. Ken asked that families be taken out of Kafakumba on the airplanes, although Lorraine chose to stay in their home. Ken agreed to stay with the village and resist. When the Army marched in, they found several hundred Africans—men and women—standing on the road. In front was Ken, tall and white, with his back turned to them, talking and laughing with his friends around him. When the captain threatened to take the village and anything his men wanted, Ken replied that he could try, but that he would be stopped. Ken refused to tell the captain how he would be stopped, but assured him that he would not take anything in the village. Furthermore, he informed the Army that they would not provide a truck to transport the Army out of the area. "The Africans stood brave as lions. They were not afraid," continued Kenny, who related the incident. The Army withdrew completely. Why? "Mental force," replied Kenny. "The fact that neither the Africans nor my father were afraid made the captain think that they knew something that the Army didn't. He may have thought that my father was too dangerous and could overpower them." Or it could have been simpler—and more complex: God intervened.

Lake Kafakumba remained home for Ken and Lorraine for the rest of their years in Congo. While they were still missionaries assigned to additional posts, Kafakumba remained an equal second site for ministries. After their retirement, they returned every year to Lake Kafakumba to teach and oversee Pastors' School. Family members and friends continued to visit them and the ministries at the site for many years. Only when civil war in 1998 forced all Methodist missionaries to evacuate from Congo did Ken and Lorraine leave Lake Kafakumba and the home they loved.

Ken and Lorraine stand in front of their home at Lake Kafakumba. By this time, the house had been enlarged, the brick covered, and rudimentary electricity and plumbing installed.

Although Ken declared war on the crocodiles in Lake Kafakumba, working diligently to keep them away from the water's edge, most got away. This one didn't, however, much to the amazement of these children.

Dubbed the Kafakumba Country Club, Ken created a simple golf course at their Lake Kafakumba home. Friends, family, and local Africans enjoyed sinking their putts on this sandy "green," as well as teeing off from the tops of anthills and taking long shots down fairways on and beside the runway. Children vied for caddy privileges and the dirt course provided Ken and others many hours of relief from stress-filled lives.

CHAPTER 5

Lubumbashi, 1966–1970

"The Lord your God is with you, he is mighty to save. He will take great delight in you, he will quiet you with his love; he will rejoice over you with singing."

—Zephaniah 3:17

After 10 years in the bush at Sandoa, Ken and Lorraine were sent to the capital of the Katanga Province and second largest city in the country, Lubumbashi. Now a city of between 1 ½ and 2 million people, it has always been the commercial heart of the region's mineral wealth. The Belgians named the city Elizabethville and reserved its central core for the residences that housed its many European citizens. The Enrights moved into a lovely home in that area, one that had belonged to a Belgian family. Lorraine was happy to be able to purchase almost anything the family needed right in the city.

The growing Methodist Church established The Methodist Centre in Lubumbashi, which housed administrative offices for the Bishop and all those overseeing the burgeoning ministries in the region. The city also became the destination for a variety of American missionaries called A-3s. A-3 was shorthand for Africa-Three Years, a program of the Methodist Mission Board that sent recent college graduates on mission assignments to Africa. Most of the young people were excellent and found themselves in life-changing ministries. Others did not fully understand the moral discipline of the African church and became troublesome to the Congolese church and community.

Lorraine remembered the Bishop asking Ken and a Congolese pastor, Matwafadi Morrison, to begin supervising the A-3 program—confirming and celebrating the work of some, while redirecting others. "Ken was loving, but he could be firm," emphasized Lorraine, as she remembered how he worked to mentor the young adults. Many of the A-3s became very good workers with pastors in local churches; indeed, Lorraine remembered Ken performing the marriage ceremony for one young couple at Mulungwishi. Marv Wolford came to Congo as an A-3 and became a lifelong friend and co-worker in ministry.

With Ken busy overseeing A-3s, preaching, teaching, flying, and continuing to lead his ministries in the Kafakumba district—including Kafakumba Pastors' School—Lorraine again found herself involved in ministries with women and children. It was here that she began to work in prison ministry, taking food for the body and food for the soul to the local prison. She organized women from different churches to cook and take food to prisoners each morning. She recalled the joy that it gave the women to do this: "Everyone loved going to the prison," she insisted—and how faithful they were to undertaking the task.

On Friday afternoons, Lorraine and others went to the prisons to conduct Bible studies and help the inmates memorize Scripture. "Matwafadi Morrison, our district superintendent, always went with us into the prisons when we held Bible studies on Friday. I always appreciated that so much," Lorraine recalled. During their years in Lubumbashi, she did not work with particular children's groups in the city. However, because children were also imprisoned (many between eight and 14 years old) these ministries benefited people of all ages.

Just as their boat, *The African Queen*, had been used to take revival meetings to the villages of the bush, Ken and Lorraine outfitted a truck in the city and used it for evangelistic meetings. "We put a piano on a truck and held services, choir and all," remembered Lorraine. They continued their work planting and founding many churches in the city, especially as the boundaries of Lubumbashi continued to expand outward. Lorraine also remembered holding many meetings in the countryside, even travelling up to six hours away to fishing villages. Ken approached evangelism in a thoughtful manner, always researching the people and getting to know their needs before entering a new area. The Methodist presence in Lubumbashi remains large today, and it continues to serve the people of southern Congo. In fact, the Conferences in southern Congo's Katanga Province have emerged as the fastest growing regions of the United Methodist Church.

By the time the family arrived in Lubumbashi, the children were scattered across the continent for their education. Oldest son, Ken, was in college in the United States and the next three children attended varied mission boarding schools in Zambia or Kenya. Only the youngest, Elinda, remained at home with her parents until she entered high school (although Kenny was home schooled until 4th grade, when he, too, left home for boarding school). The others left home at 2nd grade for the nine-month boarding school year, just as all the other missionary children did. "We were told that our children wouldn't be able to adjust and be normal if we didn't send them to boarding school," said Lorraine. At a time when few home school resources were available and families lived deep in the bush, there seemed to be no alternatives. It was difficult for everyone, parents and children alike, and made time together for the family especially precious. Perhaps it was their absence from one another that made school vacations, holidays, and summer times especially sweet at Lake Kafakumba.

Some missionary children found it difficult to fit into American culture. Ken and Lorraine did something unique, something so right, that none of their children ever felt the sense of being an outsider. All of them continue to treasure their African roots, and all remain involved in the continuing ministries their parents founded. John followed his own call into mission ministry and, except for years spent in college and seminary, has lived his entire life in central Africa. Now it is a new generation's turn to identify with their African roots. As Ken and Lorraine's grandchildren become young adults, it is clear that they, too, remain connected. Lorraine's continued commitment to her African "God's Kids," her travels back and forth between the continents, her perpetual collection of items and funds for ministry, her stories, and encouragement have left indelible marks on this new generation of Enrights. One wonders how many of them might find their lives intertwined with the beloved Congo of their grandparents.

Camp meetings

Ken and Lorraine began holding revival and camp meetings very early during their time in Congo, beginning in Mulungwishi, and continued to hold them for many years. Evangelistic services and revivals were often held in villages, generally with a pastor and church already established. Ken always believed that camp meetings were an important way to bring together the congregations of sprawling Congolese districts, uniting people around Christian fellowship, education, and inspiration. "We had services all day long and what a joy it was to see the Africans come to Christ," remembered Lorraine. Elaine, their oldest daughter, was an infant of three months the first time they held a camp meeting. She slept in the little Belgian buggy that John used when the family first arrived in Congo.

Camp meetings were held once or twice a year, generally in July or August, and usually brought two districts together. Everybody slept in simple grass houses constructed from sturdy branches planted upright in the ground and woven around and covered with long elephant grass. Missionary families brought enough food for missionary visitors and speakers and meat for the Africans who would attend. All cooking was done outside over open fires, a specialty at which Lorraine became quite adept. "We cooked soups, vegetables, and meat. We'd take Klim (powdered milk), and I would bake cinnamon rolls, cakes, and cookies to take along," she remembered. The men hunted for wild game to feed the group; hippos and elephants were especially treasured for the plentiful meat they provided.

Camp meetings lasted one to two weeks and featured both Congolese pastors from the area as well as missionaries who often travelled from the nether reaches of the South Congo Conference (then called South Shaba). One particular camp meeting/revival event featured Dr. John Wengatz—the missionary who inspired Ken to give his life to African ministry while he was still a student at Taylor University.

Days during camp meetings began early with devotions and prayer, followed by morning Bible classes. After lunch and a brief rest, the group gathered for worship until five or six—singing and preaching and studying the Bible. Evenings included huge bonfires with more singing and testimonies. Lorraine and other missionary wives often led studies for pastors' wives in varied topics that included Scripture, but might also include practical lessons in hygiene, family life, or the role of a pastor's wife in village life. Children were also included in learning and fellowship, memorizing Bible verses, songs, or stories. For all the children, missionary kids included, camp meetings were times of rollicking fun.

One camp in particular left a big impression on Lorraine: Samasan. The site was about 45 miles from Mwajinga and 30 miles north of Sandoa Post. It was beautiful with waterfalls and rapids on the Lulua River, but its road was blocked by huge lava outcroppings. This meant everyone stopped and unloaded their cars and trucks and portaged their supplies the last mile to camp. When the family arrived at Samasan, Ken didn't stop to unload the vehicle as usual. Instead, he continued driving up and over the outcroppings. Lorraine remembered her terror at the tipping car and her certainty that the family would plunge off the rocks and be dashed against the ground below. "Kenneth don't do this. Kenneth don't do this," she cried. Although Ken had calculated the angle of the huge stones and the weight of the car, his confidence escaped Lorraine. Years later, Kenny remembered that day. "My father was a wild man," he laughed. "We kids were so afraid. It looked like we were driving at 35 to 45 degrees; but, of course, my father had done the calculations and knew that we would be okay." Of all their experiences in a war-torn Congo and the many terrors of African life, Lorraine easily recalled this day as one of her most frightening. The car made it to the camp site, however, and soon others followed; they never portaged supplies at Samasan again.

Lorraine remembered many people from their years of camp meetings, but one African couple in particular became very dear to the Enrights. Pastor Silas and his wife, Mama Esther, lived in the village of Kangamba. Ken and Lorraine and their children arrived at the village very late on the night before they were to begin preparing the grounds for the camp meeting. With two little boys and their new baby girl, the family prepared to spend the night in the car. Pastor Silas came to greet them at the late hour and insisted, "You're not going to sleep in the car. You're going to sleep in our house." So, he and his wife cleared their house in the middle of the night, and the family slept in their bed. "It didn't matter what color your skin was; our desire was to do what God wanted us to do. To this day, Pastor Silas and Esther hold a very special place in the hearts of the Enright family."

John and Kendra Enright continued the tradition of these camp meetings in their years as missionaries in Congo. Their experiences with camp meetings were very similar to those John's parents experienced. In 1987 Kendra described a typical meeting in this letter to supporters:

Dear Friends,

What do you do at a camp meeting? That was what we were wondering as we started out to the Zaire (Congo) River last month for the camp meeting we had been planning. Lowell and Claudia Wertz (Lowell was Ken's nephew, making the couple John's cousins) and their two children joined our family, and we headed out to set up camp for five days. Most of the Africans had already arrived when we got there, some by truck, many by foot. There were about 200 there. All along the river, tucked in among the trees, were little "camps," which consisted of anything from a nice mattress to a reed mat to sleep on, and nearly all had some kind of a mosquito net to cover the bed, as we had all heard stories of how the mosquitoes on the Zaire River will carry off their victims! The little camps were usually a group from the same area or a family group. Each camp had a fire burning. We had purchased two cows so there was plenty of meat for everyone, and they had all brought the rest of the food supplies they would need for the stay. (Actually, the Enrights and Wertzs had tents, lawn chairs, etc. so we didn't really rough it—and the mosquitoes were essentially non-existent!)

Our daily schedule consisted of two preaching services during the day and an evening campfire service with lots of singing and testimonies. The district superintendent and several of the pastors in the area had worked with John in organizing the program and the theme for the meeting was "Growing in Christ." It was an interesting time because most of the people attending were very active Christians who just wanted to get away from the day-to-day things and spend some time studying, sharing, and praying. The evening testimony time was especially encouraging as one after another stood up to tell what the Lord had done in his or her life. The Luba tribe is known for their singing, and with three drums, rattles, etc… it was always hopping. The missionaries' rendition of "This World Is Not My Home" seemed pretty slow compared to their music.

Jesus called his disciples to go apart and rest a while in Mark 6, and we felt Him calling us to do the same as we went to the camp meeting. It was a time of real spiritual soul-searching, growth, and fellowship. Thank you for your prayers for the camp meeting and the other areas of work that we are involved with.
Together in Christ, John and Kendra Enright

Ken's preaching drew large crowds, and his remarkable storytelling was very effective in making the Bible come alive for people in both the United States and Congo.

Ken oversaw the construction of hundreds of churches during his years in Congo. Working with local pastors and congregations, he travelled frequently to check on brickmaking and building, while also raising money to provide tin roofs for the structures. Churches in remote sites required herculean efforts to deliver tin. Most remain standing and strong, although some were destroyed by war.

Handmade bricks were the foundation for all construction in rural Congo, as is the case today. Soil from anthills is most commonly used because ants remove the clay from below and deposit it in distinctive hills. Sun-dried bricks (foreground) can slump from the effects of weather unless they are cured and cared for properly. Kiln-dried bricks (a kiln is being built in the background) are much more stable and last a long time. Although grass roofs remain most common in the countryside, tin roofs are preferred for their longevity (but remain too expensive for most to afford).

Children gather whenever a camera is present. Notice the young girl already able to carry a large container on her head. Throughout her life she will carry seemingly impossible burdens of water, food, wood, thatch, and more on her head.

Girls begin to carry things on their heads at a very young age. By adulthood, women can (and do) carry almost anything on their heads.

Mission planes provided needed transportation for missionaries and others. As Lubumbashi emerged as the headquarters for the Methodist conference administration, many people flew in and out of the city. Untold greetings and goodbyes were said on the runways.

CHAPTER 6

Kolwezi, 1972–1978

*"I was hungry and you gave me something to eat,
I was thirsty and you gave me something to drink,
I was a stranger and you invited me in, I needed
clothes and you clothed me, I was sick and you
looked after me, I was in prison and you came to
visit me."*

—Matthew 25:35–36

After returning from furlough in the United States in 1972, Ken and Lorraine were assigned to Kolwezi, another large city in the region's copper belt. Kolwezi was the center for much of the region's copper mining industry and was the Katangan center for the large Inga-Shaba electric project. (This huge, long-time effort was undertaken to bring electricity from the Inga Dam at the mouth of the Congo River in the north to the resource-rich Katanga Province in the south.) Kolwezi had a large hospital funded by the huge Gecamines (the Belgian mining conglomerate that had been nationalized when Congo became independent), shopping centers, and schools for the European nationals living in the city. Although the mines had been nationalized, they remained managed by administrators and technicians from varied European countries, Australia, or South Africa. The city had a beautiful lake, golf course, stables, and other amenities that attracted many of the residents in their leisure time.

By this time, all of the Enright children were grown and gone except for 12-year-old Elinda. Kenny was married and living in Illinois, attending the University of Illinois law school. Oldest daughter Elaine was in nurse's training in Indiana (a skill she later brought back to Congo with her physician–husband, Dick). Eileen had graduated with an accounting degree from Taylor University in Indiana and was working near Washington, D.C. John had graduated from college and graduate school in Indiana and returned to Africa as a Methodist missionary. He and his wife Kendra were stationed at Luena in Congo at the time. Elinda had stayed at home through her elementary years, attended a French-speaking school through the seventh grade, and attended American schools only during the family's furloughs, which took place every four years. Later, in 9th grade, she went to the English-speaking Rift Valley Academy in Kenya, where many missionary children from central Africa attended.

Elinda had many happy memories of home life during her grade school years—memories of her father playing games with her in the evenings, driving her to school in the morning, and helping her with her studies; learning French; caring for her little garden; and playing with friends. She loved going to the French-speaking school filled with children of Belgian parents. Although she spoke little French, her first teacher was very encouraging, and before long she was just like all the little Belgian kids. She had many friends and enjoyed wonderful birthday parties with her classmates. "We thought for sure Elinda would grow up to be a teacher. She kept her school supplies in perfect order, and every day she would gather her young African friends on the porch and play school, teaching them what she had learned that day," remembered her mother. Notably, several years later, the administrator of the French-speaking school,

Mister Deporc, played an important role in the family's escape from rebel captivity during the Kolwezi Massacre.

For Ken and Lorraine, the work continued much as it had before. Again, Ken was assigned to work as a technician overseeing church construction in that region, as well as with the district superintendents in the Kafakumba and Dilolo districts. He devoted himself completely to preaching and planting churches, constructing church buildings, evangelistic crusades, revivals, training teachers and pastors, the Kafakumba Pastors' School, and the ever-present need for his skills as a pilot.

Lorraine, too, continued her ministries with young women and children. She oversaw 18 God's Kids classes and Friday Child Evangelism groups. When the groups gathered, 300 to 400 children were present. Lorraine trained women to teach the children, focusing as always on memorizing scripture and practical applications of Bible lessons. "My, those children could memorize," said Lorraine as she remembered the remarkable Congolese ability for memorizing and reciting, famed as they were for retaining their oral histories and storytelling. Lorraine smiled as she remembered: "The ladies tramped around the city listening to class members recite their verses, sometimes even at night. Ken would get upset with me for doing that, so I tried not to go out with the women after dark." Sometimes Ken accompanied Lorraine to entertain the kids. God's Kids rallies were big events; it was not unusual for a rally to have several hundred children. Ken's ability to perform magic tricks was always a big hit. (His use of magic as a medium for storytelling proved to be quite effective once everyone—including the adults—understood that magic was sleight-of-hand and not sorcery.)

Elinda remembered observing the closeness of her parents, "They just talked all the time to each other. They were very close and always had a sense of being just exactly where God wanted them to be." Onlookers might wonder how it was possible for this couple, Ken especially, to get so much done—and yet be home most evenings. His innate and well-honed people skills, his communication skills and ability with languages, his laser-like vision, sense of calling, and simply huge capacity for work set him apart in the field. Son John later spoke of his father as being "an incredibly gifted and creative person. He was truly a gifted amateur—that is, an amateur only in that he always truly loved what he did." Ken's creativity was legendary, whether fixing equipment and airplanes, dealing with government officials or recalcitrant rebels, teaching pastors, playing with his children, developing relationships, coaxing donors, or imagining new ways and places for ministry. His family sometimes shook their heads, knowing that their father's dreams sometimes meant that others had to pick up the hard work of seeing a project through to completion.

The former head of the United Methodist Church's Global Ministries, Randy Day, put it simply this way: "He was a legend in his time in Africa." The combination of Ken and Lorraine's talents and steadfast faith set the couple apart. They remain legendary figures in the growth of the United Methodist Church in Congo.

Kolwezi attracted media attention at times as the continued conflict in the country fueled one uprising after another, especially in the mineral-rich south. Lorraine vividly remembered one particular group of journalists—one English and three Spanish—who tried sneaking into Congo from Zambia, seeking news of the war. They were arrested at the border and thrown into solitary confinement in the jail at Kolwezi. When a local Catholic priest learned of the reporters' plight, he took a note to the Enright house advising them of the situation. He added that he was "not going to do anything with this; you can do what you want."

Although the family was ready to go to church, Ken decided they would visit the jail instead and see what they might be able to do to help. It was a dangerous proposition, and he instructed Lorraine and Elinda to stay close and do exactly as he said. At the jail, he told Lorraine and Elinda that if he said, "Come," they were to respond quickly, because he was going to try to get into solitary confinement and see the reporters.

And, that is exactly what happened. Ken approached the jailers and asked where solitary confinement was. Lorraine recalled the story: "The jailers pointed to a door and said, 'Right behind that door.' He turned and said to Elinda and me, 'come quickly.' Then, he shouted, 'You prisoners, where are you?' And they answered, 'We're in here.' It all happened so quickly that the jailers didn't know what to do. They let all three of us through the door, and we talked to the prisoners in their cells. We promised to come back and bring them food, water, and mattresses. We had some friends who owned a store, and they gave us whatever we wanted. The jailers said, 'You can't bring those mattresses and things in here.' But Ken said, 'These men won't be in here very long, and when they're gone, who will get to keep these things? You will!' And, the prisoners pleaded with us, saying, 'Please get word to our governments so the embassies know we need their help. We're going to be executed tomorrow.' We rushed home to our radio and connected with a lady in Zambia who had a short-wave radio. She put us in touch with the British Embassy, and they promised to try to contact the Spanish Embassy for us. The messages got through just in time, and the governments sent word not to kill the ones who were captured," finished Lorraine.

The next morning, people were sent to remove the three prisoners from the jail, and they were taken to the nicest hotel in town and given clean clothes. They were sent to Kinshasa that same day, where the immigration department agreed to let them live, promising to send them back to their home countries immediately. Several months later, the English prisoner wrote the Enrights a letter saying, "After I got out of prison I had such a terrible congestion in my chest that I had to go and spend six months on an island to get healed. I just want to take time to thank you for all that you did. God truly used you." Indeed, the prisoners owed their lives to the extraordinary quick-thinking of their missionary rescuer. That letter remains in a box of Lorraine's Congo mementos, a reminder of many other life-and-death interventions that God had performed through their lives.

In Kolwezi, Lorraine proved herself to be just as cunning and courageous as Ken had proven to be in freeing the foreign reporters from jail. Son Kenny shared a story that Africans had related to him about an incident involving the Army, a pastor, and Lorraine. One day, a contingent of 10 to 15 soldiers from military security arrested one of the Methodist pastors in the city (the military was suspicious of Lunda pastors, fearing that they might have ties with rebels in Angola). Lorraine feared that he would disappear if taken to the military prison, and this time she decided that if they were going to take the pastor away to prison, she was going to go too. The soldiers bound the pastor's hands and began to march him to the military prison; Lorraine walked right along with them. Soon a crowd of children began to run alongside yelling to the soldiers: "Why are you arresting a white woman? Where are you taking our missionary?" Before long a huge crowd had gathered and began yelling at and threatening the soldiers.

More and more adults joined the crowd, some picking up stones and bricks to throw at the soldiers. The situation was quickly becoming a riot. The captain of the contingent stopped and said to Lorraine, "Things are getting a little out of hand, please ask the crowds to go away." To which Lorraine replied "Yes, you have provoked the people and now you are going to have to respond." The captain made his decision. "I'll tell you what, Madam, if you will take him back and talk to the crowd, we will let him go and will not arrest him." So the soldiers freed the pastor, moved away, and Lorraine turned to the crowd and thanked them for their support. Then, in typical Lorraine fashion, she invited everyone over to their house to celebrate their great victory.

Ken and Lorraine always considered the well-being of women and children critical to ministry. Empowering women and nurturing children had huge effects on individuals and communities. Note how comfortable these women and children are with Bwana Ken, the white giant of a man among them.

Kids caring for kids were a common site, especially while mothers worked their gardens. Today, an increasing number of homes are classified as "orphan head of household" in Central Africa, as youngsters become responsible for siblings orphaned by AIDS.

97

African roads were always busy places. This thoroughfare accommodated cars, trucks, oxen and carts, people walking and bicycling, and children and animals of all shapes and sizes.

Ken crossing the Lulua River (1958) on a typical ferry. Large dugout canoes were fastened together and covered with a wooden deck, then ferried across the river with their loads by men using large poles. The canoes were notorious for leaking, but the greatest danger of the crossing was the possibility of falling into the crocodile-infested water. Fortunately, Ken and the truck made it across in fine shape.

CHAPTER 7

Captive in Kolwezi: May 1978

He who dwells in the shelter of the Most High will rest in the shadow of the Almighty. I will say of the Lord, He is my refuge and my fortress, my God, in whom I trust.

—Psalm 91:1–2

Background: Lorraine and Elinda, as well as John and Kendra, were held hostage in Kolwezi for seven terror-filled days by soldiers of an invading Angolan army. Their ordeal began early Saturday morning, May 11, 1978, and ended Friday evening May 17th. The week included particular horrors for the Enright family: Being taken prisoners in their home early on Saturday, the first day of the invasion, while rebel soldiers stole food, aviation gas, and other valuables; Lorraine was taken out twice on Sunday for interrogation and presumed execution; machine gun attacks almost destroyed the Enright home on Sunday evening; on Tuesday John was tried and convicted in a military court, his delivery from execution remains unexplainable; on Friday evening, May 17th, French paratroopers dropped into the center of the city, not far from the Methodist compound, and guarded it through the night. The entire week was filled with terror as the invading army disintegrated into an uncontrolled rampage against the people of Kolwezi.

Kolwezi's residents went to sleep on Friday night, May 10, 1978, as they had so many other nights. Rumors circulated that Katangese soldiers might be returning to make trouble, as they had done four years earlier in a full-out invasion that included East German and Cuban soldiers. Since that invasion, known as Shaba I, people had grown somewhat accustomed to rebel activity but took no special note of unusual activity that night. The Congolese (Zairian) army kept a small force of 300 troops in the city, hardly a contingent big enough to ward off an attack if they had believed it was about to take place. The city slept soundly, no doubt with only thoughts of the upcoming weekend to fill a person's mind.

Kolwezi residents may have been thinking about work; the city was the center for the southern portion of the huge Inga-Shaba power line being constructed in the area. The copper mines in the region were in full production, and both African workers and European management and technicians lived in the city. Some may have been looking forward to weekend recreation on a nearby lake, a local golf course, or a scheduled horse show. The population of about 2,250 Europeans and 100,000 Africans had no idea that come sun-up their world would change forever.

Ken, Lorraine, and Elinda were living in Kolwezi in 1978. Although they were still assigned to the Kafakumba district, overseeing the ministries and Pastors' School there, they lived most of the time in Kolwezi, where Elinda attended school. Having just turned 12 years old, Elinda was still able to live at home and attend a local French-speaking school. Friday was an ordinary day: Elinda went to school and made plans to be with friends on Saturday; Ken flew a group of annual conference delegates to the Methodist center at Lubumbashi and then stayed on to get some business done before the family left for their scheduled furlough; Lorraine went about her day, but was cooking a little extra food because John and Kendra had stopped to visit for a few days on their way to Lake Kafakumba for Pastors' School.

At daybreak, the Enright household was awakened by the sound of gunfire, explosions, and the noise of moving trucks. Although they did not know it, a Katangese rebel army allied with the communists in Angola had launched their attack on Kolwezi by first destroying the airport and blowing up the planes housed there. The rebels, known as Katangese "Tigers," were Congolese men from the Katanga province who had been trained under communist troops in Angola. Some had been taken by force to Angola, but some had gone voluntarily, hoping to join a military that would return and free Congo from the iron fist of Mobutu Sese Seko.

The official party name of the Tigers was the Front for the National Liberation of the Congo (FNLC), and its rebels had been wreaking havoc in the regions of South Katanga (South Shaba) for several years. Previously, this powerful force based in Angola had launched the Shaba I invasion, and communist rebels had attacked cities in the region, terrorizing the area's people with months of harassment and brutal warfare. The soldiers of Shaba I had also set their sights on mission stations and captured both Kasaji (a Plymouth Brethren site) and Kapanga (a Methodist station known for its fine hospital). It was during the three-month siege at Kapanga that a medical missionary and dear friend of Ken and Lorraine's, Dr. Glenn Eschtruth, was falsely accused of espionage and executed in cold blood. His death was a great loss to the extended mission family and to the people of the Katanga province who relied on his compassionate medical expertise. In the intervening years, the Congolese Liberation Front (including several Communist, Cuban, and East Germen military advisors) had regrouped in Angola where they were heavily supported by Cuba and the Soviet Union.

Lorraine's first thought when she heard the commotion outside that morning was of the 150 barrels of aviation gas they had stored in an outbuilding near the house. She bolted from bed and headed for the front porch, searching for the district superintendent who lived next door. When she found him she asked anxiously, "Myopo, are we at war?" The man had been awakened by the same gunfire that awakened Lorraine and didn't know any more than she did.

At the sound of gunfire, John immediately got on the radio with his father in Lubumbashi and warned him of the attack, telling him not to return to Kolwezi. Because the family had experienced other rebel attacks, John knew the guerrillas would be listening for any radio communication from the city and would hunt down any radio locations. Radios were forbidden, and their discovery could mean death for their owners—and certainly the equipment would be confiscated or destroyed. His fear was well-founded: rebels soon entered the house and destroyed the radio and transmitting equipment. Fellow missionary pilot, Harold Amstutz, lived in another part of the city and was also caught in the attack. He was able to radio news of the attack to a listener in the capital before rebels began storming his neighborhood, yelling "missionaire, missionaire." (1) The FNLC was obviously equipped with the best of directional finders, allowing them to locate and destroy all radios and transmitters in the area quickly.

Many groups of soldiers came in and out of the compound where Ken and Lorraine lived (which also included the Methodist district superintendent's home, a storehouse, and other homes on a three to four acre parcel of land) all day Saturday. They found the aviation gas, which meant that rebel soldiers were continually returning and pumping gas in their trucks. They commandeered John to do the work of transferring fuel until the entire stock was depleted.

Soldiers stormed in and out of the house without warning and at all hours, taking food, taking whatever they wanted, terrorizing the family. In a small gesture of defiance, Lorraine slipped a jar of jam into a vase, hiding it for the family's toast in the morning. She knew that these were Katangese rebel soldiers. Because the family all spoke Swahili, they were able to converse with the soldiers. John, who also spoke Lunda and Chokwe (local tribal languages), was able to communicate with everyone at every level. Lorraine wondered if some of the soldiers had been involved in the earlier attack on the Plymouth Brethern mission at Kasaji or on the Methodist missionaries at Kapanga where their beloved friend was murdered.

By Sunday, their friend and airplane mechanic, Kasanda, had made his way to the house and offered to stay and protect them. Kasanda himself was at risk because his identity card had been stolen from him and, if found without it, he would be killed immediately. On Sunday afternoon, rebel soldiers received incorrect information that Congolese soldiers were holed up in the Enright home. They subsequently attacked the house with small arms and machine gun fire. John remembered walking across the living room at one point when machine guns began immediately spraying round after round of bullets through the windows. Miraculously, he was not hit. The family dove for cover and remained barricaded in their home. An interior hallway provided the most shelter from the intentional barrage of bullets. Fortunately, the home had been built by a former missionary who took extra precautions and built the walls of that hallway with a double thickness of brick. Little did he know how those extra fire-glazed bricks would save the lives of another missionary family. With bullets destroying their home and aiming to kill them, the family huddled together on mattresses in the hallway, sleeping little. A tiny closet off the hallway also looked like a good place to hide—but their dogs had beaten them to it.

Finally, John was able to wave a flag and tell the soldiers that it was only a missionary family occupying the home. At that point, the soldiers ordered the family out of their hiding place. John slipped the key to the office door into his pocket and the family went out. For Lorraine and John, the simple acts of slipping the jam into the empty pot and sliding the key into his pocket must have been important symbolic gestures. The family was totally at the mercy of the varied bands of soldiers who filled their home.

Soldiers continued to search the house and terrorize the family in the wee hours of the night. They also looted whatever they wanted—even Kendra's diamond wedding ring. One particular night (the exact night lost in the terror of the multi-day rampage), a group of soldiers, high on drugs and alcohol, entered the house about 3 a.m. When the one lone candle burned out, casting the home into darkness, the family heard the clicks of the soldiers' rifles as they prepared to shoot. "It was simply terror upon terror," John recalled. "It was so indescribable; you kind of went into a coma because your mind couldn't handle what you were seeing: people being shot, being taken out to be killed [including both Lorraine and John], people lined up in front of our house, bombs coming in and landing, strafing by airplanes and machine guns. And, everyone was threatening to kill you five times a day." By about the fifth day, the family was totally numb from the terror.

On Sunday, the Katangese soldiers set their sights on Lorraine, ordering her to go with them to the commander of the invading army, Colonel Mofo. Knowing the danger of such an order, Lorraine replied that she did not want to go. No one knew at the time that rebel leaders were holding impromptu courts across the city and executing people they determined to be allied with the government or simply enemies of the people. The soldiers thus had no choice but to take her to Colonel Mofo. The Colonel, however, was busy, so they returned home. Lorraine always kept a little money in her pocket for tipping; she thus gave the soldiers a small amount of money. Even so, they told her that they would have to take her back to the Colonel when he was free. Lorraine spoke Swahili with their captors, which surprised the soldiers and gave her some confidence that she would not be harmed. Furthermore, one of the soldiers had an injury to his eye, and Lorraine dressed it for him.

Still, the soldiers again took Lorraine away for an audience with the Colonel. She was taken to the place where many executions of white people had taken place; the brutal killings of innocent people were later detailed in news reports, including

Time magazine. (2) However, the soldiers escorting her were now sympathetic to her. They said, "We promise you, Mama (an African term for older women), we will take you safely back to your house." When they presented her to Colonel Mofo, who was at a command post about two miles from their house, he asked the soldiers, "Who is in this woman's house?" The soldiers replied dishonestly, "Only this white-haired lady and her three kids." They used a term for children that indicated very young children, not adults. (Colonel Mofo was looking for Ken and John at this time, both of whom he knew by name.) The colonel set Lorraine free with these words: "I have nothing against her; I am not interested in a woman and her children. Take her home." The rebel soldiers took her home and asked for more money, which she was glad to give because they had saved her life.

In the chaos and the executions, it was not clear why Lorraine was not killed. Perhaps the rebels felt sympathy for her and other missionaries because of their dedication to helping people in the region. It did not hurt that she spoke Swahili, nor that she was clearly sympathetic toward and connected with African culture and life. Lorraine credited her deliverance to God—another miracle in a lifetime of miracles.

After another uneasy night on the floor in the hallway, another detachment of soldiers again entered the Enright household Monday morning. Lorraine gave them Bibles and talked to them. There had been no electricity or water since Saturday, and soldiers had stolen their food two days before. When the rebels left the house on Monday, they made sure the family had water and food; they even turned the water and electricity back on. They also made sure the dogs had enough food. "The soldiers were kind to me, and we all spoke Swahili, so it was easy to communicate," recalled Lorraine. She was counting on God and their ability to communicate with the rebels as the means of their survival. She and Kendra bantered back and forth as they cooked, trying to distract themselves from the terror surrounding them. No one was hungry and no one ate much.

The days were confusing and chaotic. On Sunday, Lorraine had been taken away for what everyone believed was certain execution, and their house had been the target of an all-out barrage of bullets. On Monday, a different group of soldiers came to their home and treated them kindly. The family never knew if their captors would be hardened Marxist ideologues intent on killing those they considered their Western exploiters, or traditional Africans in the rebel army who were sympathetic to the missionaries and their work throughout the region. As order broke down in the invading army, many small factions of rebels began drunken rampages across the city. Added to the confusion was the presence of government troops and varied security forces. The family was kept constantly on edge by the endless parade of soldiers in their home.

"But Tuesday was another day," emphasized Lorraine, contrasting its events to what had transpired on Monday. A group of African friends, including an old hunting friend from Mwinbez named Nawaej and their local pastor gathered with the family. A detachment from the military security police came into the house about four in the afternoon and ordered John to go with them. Everyone feared that John was being taken away to be shot.

The rebels left a boy-soldier to guard the family with an automatic rifle. Such boys were often kidnapped or cajoled into a junior, pioneer military service, provided with alcohol and drugs, and became known for their unpredictable violence. It was all too much for Elinda, who could not stop her tears. She cried so hard that the boy-soldier, a Congolese boy of about her age, told her "If you don't stop crying, I'm going to shoot you." Lorraine's voice reflected the stern quietness of her words, even these many years later, as she instructed her daughter, "Lindy, you've got to stop crying. God will help you." She continued, "And He did. She stopped crying immediately."

John was taken about two to three blocks to a military court to meet his rebel accusers. He remembered an encounter with soldiers the first day of their captivity. His heart sank as he recognized one of the soldiers as an old African friend from Lake Kafakumba. He knew the soldier recognized him, too. When another soldier accused him of being John Enright (although it was unclear why they were intent on killing him when they were instead searching for his father), John's friend came to his aid. "He's not John Enright. I know John Enright and this is not him," he insisted. His words saved John's life and the soldiers left.

Tuesday's ordeal, however, meant that John would face his accusers at a trial held by a Katangese officer in a small store-front-turned-courtroom. Three Africans had also been accused, and the four of them sat wordlessly on the floor. It was about seven or eight in the evening, and the room was dark. The officer heard the false accusation that John had aided government troops with his radio and ordered him to be taken out for execution. As the detachment left the court and went out to a ditch, another soldier approached and intervened. He argued with the executioners and stood between them and John, preventing them from shooting him. The unknown soldier walked with John all the way back to the house and stayed with the family for about an hour. They never knew his name. He simply sat down for a short time and finally rose to his feet, commenting, "You'll be safe now." He disappeared into the darkness, and the family never saw him again.

Lorraine remembered God's deliverance of their mechanic, Kasanda, who had also been taken away by soldiers. One of the soldiers who had been intent on killing John was also the soldier who took Kasanda's identity card a couple of days prior. When Kasanda was being accused of not having his card, the soldier inexplicably showed it to the group, who then returned it to the mechanic and thus saved his life. When the soldiers brought Kasanda back to the Enright house, they also brought a case of Johnny Walker whiskey. The Enrights have always despised alcohol. "I've always been so much against liquor, and it was an insult to have the whiskey in my living room," said Lorraine. But the soldiers left soon enough and took the alcohol with them. Before the evening ended, however, another group of soldiers invaded the home and took all their clothes from the closets. By nine o'clock the house was tensely quiet again. The family spent another sleepless night on the mattresses on the hallway floor. A somber Lorraine continued, "It was the end of a very troubled day."

The household spent Wednesday very uneasily. They had not been in contact with Ken since the morning of the invasion. And, they were unsure how long the siege would continue. They knew that the white population of the city would be evacuated—by Gecamines officials or by those in charge of the Inga-Shaba project. They knew that as American missionaries they would not be identified by these corporations. They could not make their way to the school or any other meeting place and could not contact their fellow-missionaries, Harold and Elsie Amstutz.

On Wednesday afternoon a very strange thing happened. Two very clean and nicely dressed soldiers came to their door. When Lorraine invited them into the living room, they identified themselves as Garanganzas—part of the Plymouth Brethren Church in Congo. They apologized for what was happening and asked the family not to leave the country, begging them to "stay and help them have peace in their country." The group prayed together and then the soldiers left. Again, in a city without food, electricity, or water, the family was given food and water—and, again, enough for their dogs.

As the family discussed their options, one idea was to try walking from Kolwezi to the Zambia border. Four years earlier, during the previous war, a group of Plymouth Brethren missionaries from Kasaji had walked out of Congo to Angola. (3) The group included a 90-year-old woman and veteran missionary, Granny Smith. Their walk became legendary among the people of the region, but this would not be the Enright family's path. Instead, John insisted that they not walk out, believing that God would deliver them by week's end—Friday to be exact. The decision was lifesaving, because the invading Katangese troops had amassed along the Zambia/Congo border and had large contingents along the path the family would have followed.

By week's end the family was paralyzed by the terror that had transpired. John spoke of it as an almost out-of-body experience, one of detachment, fear, and watchfulness that felt surreal. There were some Belgians living in Kolwezi at the time who had also lived through World War II. Later, they described their experiences in that war as "nothing" compared to what they went through at Kolwezi. The seven days compacted intense horror, butchery, and insanity upon the residents of the city. Kendra developed facial paralysis, a muscular tic, and the inability to speak for a time. Although tested later for multiple sclerosis, doctors diagnosed the symptoms as the result of intense stress. No one could eat (even when food was available), and they lost a precipitous amount of weight. Lorraine spent her days that week sitting on the floor, scraping up minute spots of paint that had been of no account days before. The mindless scraping gave her something to do in the midst of numbing terror.

Friday came and the atmosphere in the city became ever more dangerous as the rebel commanders began to lose control of their troops. Increasingly, both Africans and Europeans were being executed. The French were promising a rescue mission. The rebel soldiers were taking to drink or panic. The government had counterattacked (President Mobutu, a former military man, had come to Kolwezi to lead government troops) and taken back the airport on the edge of town. The situation in the city was desperate. On the previous Sunday, John heard what he clearly believed to be the voice of God assuring him that the family would be safe. He remembered the exact words, "On Friday you will be set free." By three on Friday afternoon Lorraine had run out of patience. "John, we're not free. God isn't going to deliver us," she told him. He said simply, "Friday isn't over yet." After a week of unspeakable horror, exhausted by the ordeals of near execution, and tormented by the soldier's continued presence, the family could hardly believe that deliverance would come at nightfall. But so it did.

As dusk fell on the seventh day of captivity, John heard what sounded like loud, droning mosquitoes. The buzzing surrounded them. John ran to the front door, followed closely by Lorraine. Kendra and Elinda called her back for fear of what was outside, but Lorraine and John stood on the porch and watched the parachutes of the Second Paratroop Regiment of the French Foreign Legion gliding down from the sky. In a dangerous maneuver—parachuting directly into the center of town—the Legion was convinced that such action was required to save the lives of those trapped in the city. John and his mother watched French soldiers running directly toward them and beckoned them on, knowing that there were no rebel soldiers by their house at the time. The Legionnaires arrived at the house—to the exclusion of all the other houses in the area—and informed the family, "We are here to set you free." The exact words that John had been promised echoed in everyone's minds; the family couldn't have imagined how the events of that night would unfold. With promises to get them out of the city the next day, the Legion soldiers bedded down in their yard, still littered with dead bodies from the week's fighting. Everyone breathed a huge sigh of relief and thanked God for their deliverance.

On Saturday morning, members of the Antitas family, Greek store owners in Kolwezi and friends of the family, arrived and took Lorraine, Elinda, John, and Kendra to the French school that Elinda attended. "We were told that all of the white foreigners were gathering at the school. Most of the people worked for the mines or the power line construction. They would wait there for evacuation arrangements. Everyone brought their freezers and any food that they might need," remembered Lorraine. Those working for the mines were well cared for by their employers, given rides to the airport and even given departure times. Considering how the airport had been ravaged, restoring flights and evacuating people was a huge endeavor.

Lorraine had no idea how they would get a ride from the school to the airport or how missionaries would be evacuated.

(Fellow missionaries Harold and Elsie Amstutz were able to drive their own car to the airport after they were freed. Neither family was able to communicate with the other, and each made their way out of Kolwezi by a different route.) Elinda brought her little dog with her, carrying it in her arms and keeping it close as the family wandered around the school that day. She found a schoolmate who had only the leash of his dog to remember him by. People wandered the school in shock, stunned by what they had just endured. One woman's husband had just been shot and killed that morning, and she did not want to leave without his body. Lorraine insisted that the woman go if there was a means for her to go; it was yet uncertain how the Enrights would find their own means out of the city.

Meanwhile, Ken was not sitting by idly in Lubumbashi during the week of his family's captivity. Though the messages of rape and murder coming out of Kolwezi were horrifying, he focused on what he could do from a practical perspective. He flew to rescue an African family trapped in a village behind Kolwezi and brought them back to Lubumbashi. He loaded gasoline into the plane and flew it to a government military unit near Lake Kafakumba, aiding their advance south to threaten the flanks of the rebels. He worked with the French military in intelligence and planning a rescue mission, providing them with technical details of the layout of Kolwezi. Later, when Kenny asked his father how he could function with the nightmares about the fate of his family going through his head, he said, "I could not help my family then, but I could help others. And that is what I focused on with all the discipline I could muster."

The days of his family's captivity were the loneliest of Ken's life. The moment he heard that Kolwezi was freed, he went to his army friends and asked for permission to fly in and rescue his family. "He knew one of the officers, because we had visited him many times due to the trouble in Kapanga," recalled Lorraine. This included the attack in 1974 when Katangese rebels held the mission site captive for months and then killed Dr. Glenn

Eschtruth. "He told Ken that he couldn't really give him permission, but he waved his hand and turned his back so that Ken could go," Lorraine recounted. Ken jumped in his plane and headed for Kolwezi—"Grand Central Station" was how Lorraine described it. The Kolwezi airport was a jumble of huge C-130 Hercules military transports, landing and taking off with their burdens of evacuees. The jumbo aircraft queued to land, leaving no space for the small Wings of the Morning aircraft. Ken snuck into the line anyway and landed in the shadow of the huge aircraft, cutting as invisibly as he might have done into a cafeteria line at school. When he jumped from the plane and approached the French commander in charge of evacuations, the captain became extremely angry when he learned that Ken was there to get his family. "The commander was so angry he almost exploded. He told Ken, 'The area of the city where your family was hasn't been freed yet.' And he shoved Ken and told him to wait out of his way." Lorraine continued, "But when the Lord frees you, he frees you in style."

Indeed, the commander was right. The city was still an extremely dangerous place to be. Factions of rebel soldiers remained entrenched in pockets and fighting continued between government and invading military units for several days. There were continued counterattacks, reprisals, revenge killings, and desperate, last-ditch, suicidal efforts. It was important that those caught in the violence be gathered at the French school, away from the fighting, while they awaited evacuation.

As Ken was being shoved aside by the angry French commander, he was also being watched. A man stepped up from the sidelines and said to Ken, "I am Mister Deporc, and I'm the director of your daughter's school. You flew me to safety a year ago when there was trouble in Kolwezi. Would you like me to drive you to the school where everyone has congregated? I will bring you back to the airport with your family." And with that, Ken and Mister Deporc stepped into a gleaming white Mercedes and drove to the school.

The first to see Ken as he walked through the door was a Catholic priest who couldn't believe his eyes. He grabbed Ken and lifted him up, crying, "You're dead! You're dead!" In fact, Radio Luanda, the Marxist radio station in Angola, had announced that Ken had been captured and executed as a foreign subversive during the invasion. Ken was happy to tell him that not only was he alive, but he hadn't even been in Kolwezi that week. Mister Deporc loaded up the Enright family, Elinda's little dog, and their bits of luggage into the Mercedes, and the group made its way to the airport.

The family tried to protect Elinda from the horror of the journey by blindfolding her on the drive to the airport. "What seemed like thousands of dead bodies were stacked along the roads, like cords of wood," remembered John. Bloating and decaying in the sunshine, the bodies awaited pickup by garbage trucks and disposal in mass graves. Bodies littered the roadways. The car passed an armored truck with a dead body hanging grotesquely out the window. The horrific sights and the stench of death spoke of the savagery that later became known as the "Massacre at Kolwezi."

At the airport, the family avoided the mass of people trying to get out and was quickly given permission to take off. Although Ken had flown many people out of harm's way through the years, helping many escape the clutches of dangerous rebels, never did he have more precious cargo than the evacuees on that flight. The family spent the night with missionary friends in Lubumbashi. The next morning, Ken returned to Kolwezi to evacuate African friends from the city and ensure protection for those that remained. He feared that innocent people would be swept up in troop reprisals in the weeks to follow.

The family called Kenny in Illinois to let him know they were free. Kenny had been petitioning the U.S. government to become involved in helping to free his family from the rebels. He believed his father and family were targeted for death because of their relationships with the traditional Christian chief of the Lunda area. Ken was well known and respected in the

Katanga Province and, with the African church, would oppose any communist incursion. White foreigners had been killed for far less, and Kenny knew his parents were very influential in the region. Missionaries were often targets of rebel soldiers who distrusted them for their influence on African Christians and their expertise in protecting their fellow Christians from Marxist revolutionaries. (4)

The entire family flew on to Kinshasa the next day, reuniting with many friends who had also sustained that terrible week of war. They then flew on to the United States for their scheduled year of furlough. Lorraine closed the door on their captivity in Kolwezi with these words: "It was during the time we were held hostage that I felt closest to God. At the end of each day we'd say, 'We're still alive.' We talked about leaving and walking by foot to get away; if we walked very fast we could have been in Sakaji in two days. But John said, 'I have prayed about it, and I do not think we should begin walking.' When it was all over, we learned there were landmines set all along the way, and we probably would have been killed if we had walked. Each day, committing our life to Christ, we asked God to lead. We did not know what the following days would bring, but we knew God was in control." With that Lorraine left the past to the past; God had been in control and would continue to be so. She was not afraid, and she moved on.

Endnotes

1. Learn more about the flying ministry of Harold Amstutz in his book, *Beyond the Monkey Paw: A Missionary Pilot's Story.* Word Association Publishers, 2001

2. On June 11, 1978, *Time* magazine reported the Kolwezi ordeal in an article titled, "Inside Kolwezi: Toll of Terror, Rebels are gone, but fear lingers on." The article begins with these words: "Kolwezi was a city of the dead." The article recounts how an estimated 2,000 rebels attacked the city, killing at least 80 whites and 200 blacks in a "brutal massacre." The author recounts how any discipline of the Katangese soldiers collapsed quickly after they entered Kolwezi, describing their actions this

way: "Drunken guerrillas ran amuck, shooting, killing, wounding, maiming, and raping. Then came the uncovering of horrors. Most of the slaughtered Europeans had been killed in clusters—including one group of 34 who were gunned down in a small room of a house where they had taken refuge. Bodies were left lying in the streets for days....As the stench became intolerable and the threat of a cholera epidemic grew, Red Cross officials recruited local workers, provided them with masks, and set up burial crews. Even as graves were being dug, new bodies were found several days after the fighting ended." Congolese (Zairian) forces later added to the death toll when they took suspected rebel sympathizers to a quarry outside the city for interrogation and execution.

3. For information about the attack on the Kasaji mission site and the long walk to Angola, see *No Fear in His Presence*, by David Dawson, M.D., Regal Books.

4. Kenny provided additional information about his family's ordeal during their captivity in Kolwezi. A student of African history, he understood the complexity of the situation in Central Africa. He explained that the army that invaded Congo from Angola was trained and supplied by Angola and its communist advisors in West Germany and Cuba. By advancing through Zambia rather than directly into Congo from Angola, the army was cut off from its supply line. In addition, the army had expected large towns and cities in Katanga to rise up and fight government forces with them. This did not happen, and within a few days, discipline within the ranks broke down and commanders had lost control of their forces in Kolwezi.

The attack on Kolwezi was very personal for the Enright family. They believed that rebel forces had every intention of killing Ken in the invasion. Africans later told the family that rebel forces had Ken in their sights when he took off from the airport the day before the invasion. A delay in communications prevented them from killing him at that time. Ken was a friend of the Congolese, and with them he would resist communist efforts in South Katanga. Ken, however, had no fear after this attempt to harm him and his family. Speaking on a telephone to Kenny as he flew out of Kolwezi, he emphasized that he would continue his work as before and "was not dissuaded in the least." Indeed, Ken and Lorraine returned to Congo after their year of furlough.

Kenny was also convinced at the time that his brother must have been killed in Kolwezi. He was certain that if the rebels knew they had John in their custody, they would have shot him within hours of the invasion. He could not believe his father's words on the phone that John was alive, and he asked to speak with him. His father answered, "Well, here's the corpse," and handed the phone to John. Even then, Kenny was overcome by the impossibility of what he was hearing.

Kenny credits African friends with saving his family's life. "The Africans were brave as lions. They never allowed my parents to be isolated. They knew that it was important to have people around; people who would witness and tell of any atrocities against a beloved family."

Years of constant rebel skirmishes and wars wreaked havoc across Congo and continue to do so. This aerial view shows the total destruction commonly left after rebel attacks. Ken and Lorraine's last mission assignment, Manono, has been almost totally destroyed by war.

CHAPTER 8

Moving to Florida, 1978

"The Lord will guide you always, he will satisfy your needs in a sun-scorched land."

—Isaiah 58:11

For years, Ken and Lorraine made Fort Wayne, Indiana, their home during their furloughs in the United States. After their flight out of Kolwezi in May 1978, the family returned to Fort Wayne, but found the attention they received hampered their healing. "We could not even walk peacefully down the street because people would recognize us and say, 'You are the people who were held captive in Congo.' There was always someone who wanted to hear about what had happened to us," Lorraine said of that summer. "But we needed time to heal from the experience." When John and Kendra asked the two if they would ever be interested in moving to Florida, they readily agreed. Lorraine knew she would welcome the state's sunshine. After spending so many years in the sun of central Africa, she simply did not care for the cold in Michigan or the overcast skies of Indiana. Florida would be perfect: it was the home of Embry Riddle University, where Ken received his pilot's training, and the only place the family knew outside the Midwest.

John and Kendra rented a truck, loaded their parents' posses-
sions, and drove to Florida, placing their things in storage until Ken
and Lorraine could get there. Ken and Lorraine had joyous reunions
with relatives in Michigan and Chicago that year and then drove to
the Daytona Beach area, where Embry Riddle has a campus. "Mission training doesn't teach you how to buy a house," laughed Lorraine as she remembered their experience. "We were just so
inexperienced and green at it." They found a "fine Christian" realtor and began their house hunting while the kids spent their days at
the beach. After three days of looking, they knew they had to do
something soon because they couldn't afford to continue paying for
a hotel room. The realtor had one more house to show them, newly
built and in a new development with only seven houses completed.
"The house was beautiful, but I told Ken I didn't expect to live in a
brand new house," said Lorraine. The realtor persisted, showing
them its three bedrooms, two baths, living and family rooms. They
decided that because it was available and priced in their range
($40,000), they would buy the house if the builder would take a lit-
tle more money off the asking price. Because the builder was at the
site with the realtor, he took off another $1,000 and thus sealed the
deal. Only one problem remained: Ken and Lorraine needed to get
out of their hotel and into a home immediately—by the next day.
"You just don't do that," shrugged Lorraine, "but what did we
know?" The builder and agent gave them the keys, turned on the
water and electricity, and the family moved in the next day.

For years, 921 Sandcrest, Port Orange, Florida was the state-
side center of Ken and Lorraine's ministries in Congo. After retiring,
the two made the brick ranch their primary home, but returned to
Congo every year for Pastor's School and to oversee other projects.
Having established Enright Flight Ministries as a 501(c)3 nonprofit, its address became well-known to many supporters. The
home was a collection site for whatever supplies awaited shipping to
Congo, a diner for the many family and friends who visited, and its
garage became the center of "Grandpa's Playroom." Always active
and fun-loving, this retirement home became a haven for fun activities and a place to renew between trips to Africa. "Perhaps my

father emerged as most real in his role as grandfather," remembered John. Ken always loved to play—with his own children, with others' children, even as part of his work and ministry. But he especially loved playing with his grandchildren. He hung a trapeze from the ceiling of the radio room at Lake Kafakumba for grandsons, Nathan and Brian, to play on. But Port Orange sported much more—a jungle gym, a fort, and games—and became the epicenter for Enright fun. Here, even as he came and went to and from Africa, Ken found great pleasure in the joy of his beloved grandchildren's company.

Eventually, even this modest home became too much care for Ken and Lorraine. Daughter Eileen and her family lived nearby and built an apartment onto their home for her parents. It remains Lorraine's home for the half year or so that she is in the United States. Florida remains home to two of the other Enright children. Oldest daughter Elaine lives near West Palm Beach with her family; youngest daughter Elinda lives with her family near Melbourne, where her husband is a United Methodist pastor (although they will be moving soon). It is an easy drive down the Atlantic shoreline to visit family members now. With Kenny and his family in Illinois, and John and Kendra's family in Zambia, Florida has become the site for annual reunions of the expanding Enright families. For Lorraine, the family's move to Florida has been simply "marvelous." She often looks at the bright sun and the blue sky and thanks God for the beautiful day. Her apartment continues to fill with supplies she will be taking back to Zambia on her next trip; friends and family still gather at her table; children and grandchildren come and go (and she keeps stock of special treats they love); and Lorraine remains steadfast in her belief that she is exactly where she is supposed to be, doing exactly what God wants her to be doing. God's presence with her remains just as sure as it was 80 years ago when she gave her eight-year-old life to His service.

Neither Ken nor Lorraine ever retired from their work. In advancing years, they continued to divide their time between Lake Kafakumba, Congo and this home in Port Orange, Florida—always returning to Congo for the months of Pastors' School and then speaking, collecting goods, and raising funds among churches in the United States. They were in Zambia for Pastors' School at the time of Ken's death in 2006. Lorraine continues to return to Zambia to oversee and teach her beloved God's Kids, a network of children's clubs around the Kafakumba Training Center. The Port Orange home was a center for their state-side ministries supporting Pastor's School, as well as a favored gathering spot for family and friends.

CHAPTER 9

Manono, 1980–1987

*He who oppresses the poor shows contempt for their
Maker, but whoever is kind to the needy honors God.*
—Proverbs 14:31

The massacre at Kolwezi, and their time of captivity and
near-death, never deterred Ken and Lorraine from returning to
Congo. Kenny believes that his parents' return to Congo after
their captivity at Kolwezi (and, later, their near-fatal airplane
crash) had a powerful impact on the people his parents served.
Because of their absolute belief that God was leading them and
their security in His will, Ken and Lorraine returned to places of
terror. Folks with less assurance would never have returned.
They did not allow a lifetime of love and commitment to be
shortchanged by a group of angry rebels and political upheaval.
And so, Ken and Lorraine left their lovely home and much-
loved families in Florida and returned to Congo after their year
of furlough following Kolwezi.

It is the practice of Global Ministries (the mission arm of
the United Methodist Church) to assign missionaries to particular geographical regions, called conferences. Missionaries serve
under the authority of the bishop of a particular conference and
do not move across borders into another conference except

under special circumstances. It is extremely rare for a pastor or missionary to be assigned to a different conference and bishop, but that is exactly what happened when Ken and Lorraine returned to Congo. For years, they had served the South Congo Conference (called South Shaba during Mobutu's rule) in the southern region of the Katanga Province. After the family was taken captive in Kolwezi, however, African Lunda and church leaders insisted that the two be moved hundreds of miles away from the Kolwezi area; indeed, they feared Ken would be assassinated by the Congolese Liberation Front. They were careful not to broadcast Ken's whereabouts, and the Luba tribesmen in the Manono region became very protective of his ministries there. Lorraine also saw the move as a way to place missionaries in a place to which others found it difficult to travel. "Two other missionary families had been assigned to Manono, but neither managed to get there," remembered Lorraine. "Our bishop sent us there, and we arrived within two weeks after being told to."

This time they had another family member in tow: Lorraine's beloved mother, Esther. And how did this grand lady from Hillman, Michigan, adjust to life in equatorial Africa? Splendidly! "She was surrounded by people who loved doing what she loved doing most—going to church. She had African women who became dear friends and who cared for her through her years of declining health and eventual death," explained Kenny. Esther Christine Lundeen Farrier proved herself very resilient in old age. "There really wasn't anybody left in Hillman who could take care of her," said Lorraine, "and so she came to Africa with us."

On one particular trip to Kafakumba Pastors' School in 1981, Ken and Lorraine stopped with her mother to visit John and Kendra at their Luena mission station. Ken's nephew, Lowell Wertz (a fellow missionary in the country), was also there with his wife, Claudia. Lorraine knew that her mother's health had been failing, and she sensed that the end was near. She asked everyone to surround her mother's bed, and when asked why, she asked for prayer, because she knew that death was imminent.

"My mother died very peacefully right there at Luena," smiled Lorraine.

The mining company stocked beautiful caskets and helped them get everything arranged for the funeral. The family decorated with bougainvillea and held the service at the Luena Methodist Church. Lorraine, however, was not able to attend the funeral. She became very sick with the flu and then had an adverse reaction to a shot that she was given. Lorraine became so sick that for a time she thought she, too, was going to die. After further treatment, she started feeling better, and she and Ken made their way on to Pastors' School. The local church at Luena has kept its promise to maintain and care for Esther's grave.

Manono is located in a region known as "Hot Africa." It is lower in elevation than the Katanga Plateau, and the equatorial heat of the region is infamous. Almost everyone who came to Manono talked about its oppressive, almost unbearable, heat. "Passengers flying in with Ken would always remark that they had a hard time breathing in the intense heat," said Lorraine. "He would continually assure them that they were almost on the ground and that they would be able to catch their breath when they landed." There was no seasonal break; the temperatures never subsided, and it was hot all year-round.

Manono was a tin mining town with many European residents working in the mining industry. "It was a very beautiful city, laid out beautifully with boulevards and palm trees. It was just the most beautiful city I'd ever seen," remembered Lorraine. The head of the local mine was a Belgian, and his wife was English. They became good friends, as did many other of the European mining families. Lorraine especially enjoyed the company of Dora, a Greek woman who ran a local store with her husband. Because of the expatriate and mining communities, Manono had stores, and Lorraine could buy most of their groceries and needed supplies right in the city.

But not all of Manono's residents were privileged. The region's poverty proved to be the most heart-wrenching that Ken and Lorraine had seen. The region was filled with hungry and homeless children, orphans so destitute that the region was dubbed "the place that children go to die." Just as she had at her previous locations, Lorraine opened her heart and home to the region's children. Again, she started feeding children daily at her doorway, just as she had at Kafakumba. "My mother was like a serial grandmother," laughed Kenny, as he described Lorraine's lifetime practice of loving every child she met.

The feeding time, with its crowd of starving children, became such a difficult experience for Ken that he could hardly bear to observe them coming to the door. "It kills me to look at the little kids each morning that line up for food. So, I just don't look at them. I hire all the women and pay them to work for a half day on the airstrip or at the garden. Thus, they can eat and pay for their treatment (at the dispensary)," Ken wrote to daughter Elinda one day. Of course Ken looked at the children in the streets and at his doorway; he saw their distended, hungry bellies and hair reddened by starvation-induced kwashiorkor. He and Lorraine looked so closely that they developed a partnership with the humanitarian group, International Christian Aid, to continue the work of feeding and caring for Manono's children after Ken and Lorraine were gone.

A new people-group emerged at Manono: the Twa, commonly known as Pygmies. Lorraine will never forget the first Sunday she and Ken went on a motorcycle to minister with the Pygmies. These tiny people of the forest were very suspicious of whites—European or otherwise. However, they soon learned that the giant of a man named Ken was indeed a friend, and that he genuinely wanted to help them. "Generally they didn't let whites near," remembered Lorraine. But the Pygmy group was very responsive to God's Word, and Ken helped them build a church and find a pastor. The pastor made his rounds to church and parishioners on a tiny bicycle. One time he had a flat tire and Lorraine recalled how methodically the little man went about fixing his tire and continuing his business as pastor. "Their pastor did a good job. He even started a school and continued to do very well," she added.

One time, a little boy in the community was dying of rabies. Ken brought a doctor (his son-in-law, Dr. Dick Fisher, who was serving as a mission doctor in Manono at the time) to care for him while he flew to Nairobi to pick up vaccine for the child. Although the boy was beyond treatment, the pastor and his wife took the child into their home and then cared for him in the forest until he finally died. And then war came again. The last time Lorraine heard of this congregation (and others) she learned that Burundian soldiers had arrived and taken everything away, just as they had to all the residents of the area. "I can't tell you how terrible they were," she said of the savagery unleashed on Manono.

Transportation was always a challenge in Congo. Just as airplanes became a lifeblood for ministry, so too, were boats for communities located near rivers. Ken was known for using whatever means possible to take the Good News out to people. Just as he had equipped a truck with a piano, preacher, and choir to take out on gospel runs in Lubumbashi, he also now envisioned another boat on the Congo (Lualaba) River. (1) He and Lorraine had successfully used *The African Queen* during earlier years of ministry. Unfortunately, rebels had destroyed that boat, so John went about building another one for shared ministry with his parents in the Luena area. Christened the *Kipendano*, it proved to be effective in living up to its name, "Love one another."

Ken and Lorraine often made their home on the boat for three- to four-day periods. Sometimes they took a nurse and another local pastor. They would anchor the boat at little settlements and ask if the people had a church. If the answer was yes, then they would go to the church and hold revival services. A pastor from the area, Kasongo Munza, would generally preach, as would Ken who also spoke in local languages. "We went and witnessed to the people who lived along the shores of the river. The fishing in that river was unbelievable. And, it truly was the way Africa used to be—unspoiled," remembered Lorraine.

The river ministry and the use of the *Kipindano* for evangelism was a joint venture between Ken and Lorraine and their missionary son John and his wife Kendra. John and Kendra were assigned to the Methodist mission station at Luena, which was in the same north Katanga region as Manono. The two couples spent much time using the *Kipendano* for ministry in settlements along the Congo River. Although the settlements were "out in the middle of nowhere" (Lorraine's description), two men who played major roles in developing Kafakumba Pastors' School hailed from the region: Pastor Kasongo Munza taught in, and would become the director of, Kafakumba Pastors' School, and John Kayeye was the engineer who later built much of the school's campus in Zambia. Fellow missionary Lena Eschtruth also made trips on the *Kipendano* as she vaccinated children in villages along the rivers.

Their assignment to Manono was full-time and there was unbelievable need in the region. However, Ken and Lorraine were also assigned to their previous district of Kafakumba and all the ministries there, including continued leadership of Kafakumba Pastors' School. Ken had his plate full but wrote about Lorraine's ministries during those years in this letter to supporters:

> *"Lorraine's outreach encompasses a feeding center, two schools, two dispensaries, and a medical depot. These ministries are 500 miles apart and work among four tribes. That stretches one lady pretty far and multiplies the demands on her heart, time, and funds. It can be very tiring! But she always goes back. Every evening she's in the sick compound trying to mother whole families into health and the Kingdom of God."*

By this time, the pair found themselves alternating between their homes and places of ministry, staying about two months at each mission site. It had always been their practice to mentor African leadership for whatever work was needed, and it became necessary to rely on African co-workers to carry out all ministries during the frequent absences of these years. Fortunately, John and Kendra lived at Luena, about midway between Kafakumba and Manono, allowing Ken and Lorraine to stop and see them in their travels back and forth between mission stations. Like Manono, Luena was very hot, so Lorraine and John had a long-running battle over which was the hotter of the two places.

In 1987, Ken turned 65 years old and Lorraine 63. They had been missionaries for 38 years, with 37 of them spent in Congo. It was time to retire—at least officially. Unofficially, they never retired. The difference was that they more evenly divided their time between Florida and Congo, between ministries in the US and ministries in Congo, between family on one side of the ocean and family on the other.

After Manono

Although Manono was their final mission assignment, Ken and Lorraine continued to return to Kafakumba for Pastors' School each year after retirement. They considered Africa—Congo in particular—their assignment for lifetime ministry. "It's been a wonderful life," insisted Lorraine, "God has been so good to us. I am so thankful to God for how he directed our lives. We didn't quit and run home, but we saw it to the end." Their love for the people of Congo never diminished, and their passion for village pastors and their churches never flagged.

Lorraine was always quick to credit Ken with their fruitful ministries. "People always responded to Ken, and he took this very seriously. He didn't go hide in the closet when people were around. He was ALWAYS a part of any situation." There is no doubt that Ken was a prodigious worker, and his role in evangelism, church-building, humanitarian flight ministry, education, health care, administration, and fund raising can never be underestimated.

Although Lorraine appeared quietly behind Ken's ebullient personality and speaking abilities, her role was equal to Ken's. She set up housekeeping in some very inhospitable surroundings, cared for and taught their children, supported Ken in all of his work, and maintained a home where all were welcome. In addition, her formal mission assignments included teaching, sometimes in schools she started, mentoring young women, and working with children. Her early interest in nursing proved to be helpful when illness and injuries presented themselves, which happened often, especially after Ken began flying medical patients. Her recognition of the important role of women as central to their homes, churches, and communities has been confirmed by many in recent years. In fact, work with women has been credited as being one of the most powerful aspects of Kafakumba Pastors' School because of its huge effect on so many people.

Lorraine had a special love for adolescent girls, and her lifelong commitment to children has been credited with saving many children's lives. "Give my mom credit," said John. "She always understood that her work with children was important. These kids, many molested and exploited, needed this base." John was referring, of course, to the love and learning that came with her God's Kids clubs. In reflecting on his parents' work, John likened their impact to that of the Impressionist painters and their paintings. "They were very ordinary people, yet they produced greatness." Who can argue with that?

As Congo's violent wars dragged on, as militias continued to terrorize the people, as roads became impassable because of roadblocks and continual violence, and as access to supplies and transportation became almost impossible, Ken and Lorraine knew they had to leave Congo for good. Many times they were held at gunpoint, had their home ransacked, faced down drunken soldiers, and had their lives threatened by the growing hostilities of war. It was the late 90s, and Congo was being gutted by violence without and within. The final trip from Lake Kafakumba was a harrowing experience that left Lorraine shaken.

The plan was simple: A fellow Wings of the Morning pilot would fly them from Lake Kafakumba to Lubumbashi, the largest city and commercial center of the region, and then they would be driven across the border into Zambia. A smooth escape depended on whether or not rebels or army soldiers would be present; Ken and Lorraine had heard that the army was in Lubumbashi and prayed that God would smooth the way for them.

The day of their departure began badly: a contingent of soldiers came to their house to harass and prevent them from leaving. Lorraine described the group's leader as a "terrible, terrible man" and one who was "really cutting the capers." The man was angry, drunken, and threatening the pair at gunpoint. He was demanding their radio and preparing to ransack the house of all its belongings. Lorraine believed that they might actually be killed by his violence. Neither Ken nor the Wings of the Morning pilot tasked to fly them out were able to calm the man. Finally, Ken called the political leader of the Kafakumba-Sandoa District to come to their aid. When the man arrived and saw the plane ready to go, he asked to speak with the pilot. "What's your mother's name?" he asked the pilot, confirming that the pilot was indeed his own nephew. The district leader confronted the angry man, and his presence allowed the plane to take off safely. The drunken soldier who threatened them was later hauled off by villagers, beaten, and sent on his way. "That was the Lord," insisted Lorraine. "The Lord took over and we had a wonderful flight," she continued.

The Army was not at Lubumbashi as they had expected, and so they were met by a large group of friends at the airport. "It was a real joy at Lubumbashi when we left; we had such a happy time with friends before leaving," remembered Lorraine. The pair was then driven to Kitwe, Zambia, and after enjoying a fine meal with their pilot's family, they were taken on to Zambia's capital, Lusaka. After their terrifying departure from Lake Kafakumba—the last time they would ever see it—Ken and Lorraine were looking forward to their return to the United States.

The flight out of Lusaka proved to be much harder to catch than they had anticipated. Airline officials told them that it was a very difficult time to be getting out of Zambia and that they should prepare for at least a two-week wait. "We didn't have any money to stay in a hotel," remembered Lorraine. The two had left Kafakumba with only the personal belongings that would fit in suitcases on a small airplane, and little cash. Again, as they had experienced so many times in the past, Ken and Lorraine knew that God would work out their departure in some unknown way. They spoke to a woman at British Airways, wondering if it would make any difference, considering the many that had been waiting for days to depart. At the same time, Lorraine's sister-in-law, Dorothy Farrier, contacted her nephew who worked for British Air. He was able to procure tickets for the pair, and in short order the same woman with whom they had spoken earlier ushered them to a separate room. "You are on the next flight out of Zambia and will be flying straight to the United States," she told them.

And so it was that this final journey, a miraculous escape really, became another example of God's protection and provision for Ken and Lorraine. They had come to recognize God at work in their lives and expected that God would work out the seemingly impossible problems around them. They knew it was God who had provided safe passage away from Lake Kafakumba and out of Congo; who had provided friends along the way; and who had provided a ticket for immediate flight out of Zambia. They considered the people involved as instruments of God's grace and much-loved gifts to them. Ken and Lorraine wondered how they could ever thank God and others enough.

Afterword

Although Ken and Lorraine left Congo for good on that day in 1998, their ministries remain very much alive. Congregations they started remain strong, and churches remain standing. Their remarkable collaboration with able Congolese allowed for the transfer of leadership in the aviation ministry, schools, health dispensaries, feeding programs, and church growth and administration. The focus of their ministries—pastoral support—remains strong in the continued growth of Kafakumba Pastors' School.

Lorraine continued her commitment to children when they moved their ministry center to Zambia after evacuating from Congo. She always believed that giving something of Jesus to broken children was the gift of a lifetime. She continues to travel to Zambia every year for about six to seven months to oversee her God's Kids Clubs, which provide love and learning for about 500 children. She also works with the children of pastors who come with their families each year to Pastors' School.

Lorraine intends to remain in Africa as long as possible. "I'm so glad Ken could die in Africa, and I want to die in Africa too—Lord willing and the creek don't rise," she says. A smile crosses Lorraine's face when she speaks of Africa. "That's the place to be," she says softly, "for us, you know."

Endnote

(1)   The mighty rivers of Congo, and their many tributaries and waterways, provided the only access to many people throughout the region. Villages large and small dotted the water, with their people eking out a living from the fish pulled from the river or from food grown on small farming plots. The first boat Ken and Lorraine used was *The African Queen*, a smallish boat (5 meters long, 5 tons in weight) that had travelled well during their years in South Katanga but was eventually destroyed by rebels. Years later—when Ken, Lorraine, and Elinda lived at Manono—John built another boat for ministry, the *Kipendano* (Swahili for "love one another" or perhaps more literally, "The Boat of Love"). It was a larger boat (15 meters long and 40 tons in weight) created by mounting a shipping container onto the boat itself. The container created sleeping space (cramped though it was), with windows and simple mattresses; generally the women slept in the container. The men (including those helping to crew the boat) slept under the container in space that created a small hold and cramped sleeping quarters. The boat included a simple kitchen and cooking space, as well as stor-

age, the refrigerator (more often used to keep vaccines cool), a generator, and other supplies. The toilet was perched off the back of the boat over the water. Painted red, the *Kipendano* became an unmistakable presence on the Congo (Lualaba) River. It motored to villages, inaccessible by roads, where people gathered to hear Ken preach; sometimes there were churches already present in villages, sometimes not. Children gathered around when the boat arrived to participate in Bible School or to get immunized. Often the revivals lasted for days, with Ken and Lorraine and others living on the boat. Sometimes the *Kipendano* was used to transport goods and supplies. Toward the end of its life, the boat started to carry some of the region's salted fish, a move that hastened its demise, as the salt caused its metal parts to erode in the hot, humid sun. The boat remains beached in the river village of Mulenda, where, no doubt, the locals have put it to some good use.

Feeding hungry people has been an important part of almost all ministries in Congo, especially for children who are chronically malnourished. There were 150 children in line for lunch the day this picture was taken.

This mother was too sick to nurse her baby, so Lorraine made a bottle for the little one three times a day.

Thousands of children have been touched by the love of God through Lorraine's Kids Clubs. "Oh my, could they ever memorize verses," she marveled.

133

Kasongo Munza (center) was a beloved friend and the director of Kafakumba Pastors' School for many years until his death in 2005. He provided leadership at both the Congo and Zambia campuses of Pastors' School.

The boat, The *Kipendano* (Swahili for "love one another"), was used to provide ministries to people along the many rivers of the region. It was a joint ministry of Ken and Lorraine and their son John and his wife Kendra (fellow missionaries). It took the families out on evangelistic crusades, medical missions, supply runs, and more.

CHAPTER 10

Flying

"If I take the wings of the morning, and dwell in the uttermost parts of the sea, even there shall Thy hand lead me."

—Psalm 139:9-10

It was during their furlough in 1960 that Ken was introduced to the idea of flying as part of his work in Congo. One day while attending a U.S. regional conference on mission, he found himself sitting next to a national church leader from the Methodist mission board, Global Ministries. The man told Ken that many of the ministries in Congo were threatened by closure if they couldn't find planes and pilots. In a country about the size of the United States east of the Mississippi River, with terrible—or nonexistent—roads and vast distances, airplanes became essential to mission work. This lack of roads, or their impassability during the long rainy season, combined with the limited usefulness of boats or trains to move people around in the huge expanse of Congo's interior, all led to a dreadful disconnect that threatened the growing Methodist churches in the region.

Just mentioning the need for airplanes and pilots was all it took to send Ken to flight classes, which he started close to where the family was staying near Chicago. Soon the Enright family found themselves at Embry Riddle Aeronautical University in Daytona Beach for several weeks of classes and tests as Ken pursued his pilot's license. Lorraine remembered it this way: "Once Ken was in an airplane that was the end of it. He loved it; just loved it. He took to flying like a duck to water." (Or maybe more like a bird to the air.) Ken proved to be an extremely skilled pilot and absolutely fearless in the air. He loved flying for the rest of his life. He often referred to flying this way: "The plane is my home, my office, my chapel."

During the family's times in the States, Ken flew to many of his speaking engagements; it reduced his travel time and kept his hours in the air current. He got to know airplane manufacturers, mechanics, pilots, and benefactors who would continue to support the flying ministry he founded with fellow missionary pilot Paul Alexander: Wings of the Morning. In 1963, he received his first plane in Congo. Later, he recruited other pilots to Congo, some of whom have given their lives to flight ministry, as well as mentored Congolese pilots who have since taken over the Wings of the Morning. (1)

The early years of flying were admittedly difficult. Remote sites required air strips—villagers built grass and dirt runways using hoes, shovels, and wheelbarrows. Without payment, the local people then maintained the strips as well. Eventually all larger villages—and some small ones—had their own airstrips, and Ken could fly throughout the whole area. The costs of airplanes and fuel were expensive, especially when flying conditions meant that a few planes ended up damaged in accidents. The program required constant fundraising from supporters in the United States. Soon everyone recognized that air travel was the only way to move people and goods needed for survival around the scattered Methodist mission stations and among the churches and hospitals, schools and cities. The airplanes were—and remain—a life blood for ministry in Congo.

Along with airplanes came a new rhythm to missionary life. Each station received a two-letter moniker; for example, Kafakumba became number 21, Sandoa number 22, and Kolwezi number 41. Wives of pilots took on the duties of flight following, staying in contact with their husbands on radio frequencies during their time in the air. Sometimes the wives would pass on flight-following duties to others along the flight path as the planes travelled throughout the region. Without flight towers or necessary instrumentation, the Wings of the Morning pilots flew using landmarks such as rivers, villages, odd-shaped fields, or mission stations. The smaller planes were prohibited from flying after dark; therefore, most pilots were home by late afternoon to beat the early equatorial nightfall at 6 p.m. Huge tropical storms (with its humidity and heat, Congo has more thunder storms than anywhere on earth) and vast stretches of remote grasslands, forests, and mountains made flying an adventurous but risky endeavor.

The mission stations stayed in regular contact with each other using ham radio frequencies. Dr. Glen Eschtruth set up a radio network among all the mission stations, including those in other regions and including mission sites sponsored by other church groups. The missionaries checked in with each other at regularly scheduled times (generally at 8 a.m. and sometimes up to three times a day: morning, noon, and 5 p.m.). Many of the conversations focused on the ordinary events of mission life: locations of personnel, need for and delivery of supplies, coordination of the people and their needs to carry out ministry. Some found it a necessary relief from the isolation of station life, with wives sometimes chatting with others living at different stations. Sometimes, the radios meant simply asking for pineapples from Kapanga in exchange for papaya from Sandoa. But often the radios were lifesavers—calling for airplanes to retrieve the sick and dying who needed a doctor, evacuating people from danger as soldiers threatened villages and mission stations, even saving the lives of those caught in rebel attacks.

It is impossible to underestimate the effect of flying on mission life. Ken and other mission pilots were on-call all the time, and they received calls for emergency flights at all hours. The Enright children remembered holidays and family times being interrupted by urgent needs for an airplane. Generally, the flights were needed for medical emergencies: a woman unable to deliver a baby, a man shot, a child with grossly broken bones or caught in the deadly grip of fever. With so few hospitals and clinics, and the distance between them amounting to hundreds of miles, airplanes were a lifesaving ministry of mercy.

Ken flew almost every day, often providing basic emergency medical care as well as flying the airplane itself. The planes were also used to transport missionaries, educators, doctors, pastors, church administrators, and others involved in the ministry of the Methodist Church in the region. An entirely separate book could be written about Ken's flying ministry, the lives changed—even saved—by his aviation skills, about God's blessing on Wings of the Morning, and the continued work of Methodist pilots in Congo. Indeed, the joy of telling those stories will be left to others. (One such book is *Beyond the Monkey Paw, A Missionary Pilot's Story* by fellow missionary-pilot, Harold Amstutz; Word Association Publishers, 2001.)

Ken's skill became legendary in Congo and in extended mission circles. He feared nothing: not the towering storm clouds that gathered in the late equatorial afternoon, nor the endless miles of grasslands beneath him; not threatening government officials nor menacing rebels whose insanity made others fear for their lives; not the precariously kept village strips in remote sites nor the dangerous airstrips in some cities; not the mayhem of war nor the sheer exhaustion of continual flying while also serving full-time in ministry with the poorest and neediest on the planet. Ken simply loved flying. It became second nature to him. In truth, airplanes became an extension of his very body and ministry.

Pilots sometimes found themselves endangered because of their influence and the high regard in which they were held by the people they assisted. Sometimes they were also accused of being part of assisting whichever enemy was in vogue at the time—whether it was America's CIA, Mobutu's regime, or some other perceived enemy of whichever rebel faction was in control at the time. The decades after Independence were very dangerous years to be serving in the country.

Because of their ability to transport people and goods, pilots were always in danger of accusations of collusion. They were feared by those seeking power, whose reasoning sometimes escaped any human understanding. Sometimes technical misunderstandings arose; one pilot found himself accused of having machine guns mounted on his plane when the apparatus was actually the airspeed indicator tube sticking out of the wing. Soldiers at some airstrips tried to extort money from the pilots, much as they did at road blocks. Hassles with customs, luggage, permission for flight—all were par for the course. At times, pilots were arrested when they landed in the larger cities; sometimes they were kept from flying for a short time or required a visit from a provincial official to gain their freedom.

In one letter, Lorraine wrote home, "When dad flew into Kabalo Monday, he was promptly arrested by the soldiers, who were drunk. They said, 'Don't you know this is a war zone?' When he first landed he wasn't sure if they were friend or foe. The soldiers bicycled in to get a signature in order for him to leave. After an hour Dad was in the air again."

Another incident happened when Ken and Lorraine were living in Manono. Ken flew out on what he thought would be a 20-minute mission. Instead, when he landed he was met by a drunken soldier with an itchy finger on his rifle. His behavior was so dangerous and bizarre that Ken had to again get help from a government official in the city. The incident stretched into hours. "I remember those times so plainly. I walked the floor. I had tense moments, very tense moments, when Ken was flying," admitted Lorraine.

Fellow Wings of the Morning pilot Harold Amstutz admired Ken's fearless approach to flying. In his book, *Beyond the Monkey Paw*, Harold told the story of the day Ken and fellow missionary pilot Don Watts flew into Wembo Nyama mission station to evacuate the wives of missionaries being held by Simba rebels. (2) Lorraine begged Ken not to make the flight.

She knew that he had never flown to Wembo Nyama before and could easily become lost over the region's unforgiving jungle. In fact, it was Ken's first time flying in Central Congo, which was huge, uncharted territory for him (his area for flight was further south in the Katanga Province). He stayed in constant radio contact with Don and followed him to the station. Harold described it this way:

They decided that Don would land first and Ken would circle overhead the strip as Don loaded his group of ladies in the plane. Then Ken would land. Ken watched the action from above. Things did not seem to be moving along very quickly. He wondered what was going on, and what was taking place. Don was finally able to get the ladies into his plane and then he called Ken on the radio.

He told Ken that the rebels said that he would have to land and that if he did, he might have to stay awhile. Ken told Don to tell the Simbas that he would have to taxi to the end of the runway so that Ken would have room to land. The rebels did not see through what they were planning. They agreed for Don to taxi to the end of the runway. As Ken landed and rolled towards the other end of the runway, he spun the plane around several times, kicking up a lot of dust. While he was doing this, he told Don on the radio to take off through the dust and over him. Don did this, and he was on his way back to Katubue (mission station). Ken then taxied up to where the rebels and the other missionaries and ladies were standing. This action took the rebels by surprise.

They were a little shocked at what had just taken place. Ken stopped his plane and got out. He started talking to the rebels in Swahili. This dumbfounded the rebels, and they started saying to each other, "Where did they get a pilot that talks our language?" This was

Otetela country and the people here spoke the Otetela language. Ken started joking with them and was doing coin tricks for them. He got them to laughing. Ken was saying, out of the side of his mouth to the ladies, "Get in the plane; get in the plane."

Ken pulled some money out of his pocket and gave it to the rebels. He also told them that they were soldiers, and soldiers keep their word. Soldiers were good people, and that Dr. Hughlett was his brother. (Dr. Hughlett was a missionary doctor being held captive at Wembo Nyama.) If the rebels hurt Dr. Hughlett, Ken said, he was going to get mad at them, because he was his brother. They told Ken, 'Oh no, we will not hurt him.' Ken told them that he was going to leave now. They agreed to this, so he got into the airplane and started it. The thought ran through his mind, 'What if the engine does not start?' But it did, and he took off.

Ken was running short of fuel. He had flown to Wembo and circled for quite a long time before landing. Now he had one and a half hours to fly back to Katubue. He did not have any maps, since he had followed Don Watts to Wembo, and he had not been in the area before. It was also getting later in the afternoon. He just prayed that God would help him get back to Katubue, and that he would have enough fuel and enough daylight left to make the flight safely. God did answer his prayer, and he did make it back safely. All the women—Mildred Lovell, Elaine Crowder, Sally Pliemann, Violet Hughlett, and Carol Siksay—had been evacuated safely. ...That evening they had a prayer service and gave God all the praise for the safe evacuation.

In just this one short story, one can glimpse Ken Enright in action: The flight into a strange location to evacuate missionaries (an activity he did many times over the years), his quick thinking to get Don and his passengers into the air by creating a cover of dust, his Irish charm and intuitive personality turned full-force on rebel soldiers, loading passengers quickly while distracting soldiers with conversation, pleading for a man's life, and persuading soldiers to let him take off against their will. Ken earned his reputation as a quick and creative thinker, as well as a skilled negotiator and pilot.

Then there was the issue of his flight out of the strange territory, flying with no maps and barely enough fuel and daylight to make the trip. Or the many times he faced murderous soldiers at gunpoint at city airports. Or flying into hostile places to rescue hostages from rebel armies. Or the undercover flight into Kolwezi to rescue his family from a bloody massacre. Most would call their deliverance from such danger miracles; Ken and Lorraine certainly did. At the end of many days, they simply thanked God, called it a day's work, slept for the night, and carried on while Ken climbed back into the cockpit the next morning.

Ken also oversaw building and maintaining dozens of grass airstrips throughout the Katanga Plateau. He built hangars and fixed his own planes and was always generous with his time to help other pilots with their needs. He befriended the aviation experts, company pilots, government officials, and anyone else who loved flight as much as he did. During his years in Congo, Ken logged 18,000 hours in an airplane—nine working years if one figures spending a full 40 hours a week in the air. It remains an awesome record. Along with his faith and family, flying became one of the greatest loves of his life.

Come With Me in a Sky So Blue

Come with me in a sky so blue
Where you have absolutely nothing to do
You smile at God and He'll smile at you
Come, won't you come with me.

Come with me in a sky so blue
Share with the Lord a wonderful view
You nod at the clouds and they nod at you
Come, won't you come with me.

Come with me to a jungle so green
Where God's at work in an African scene
Join our trip on the African Queen
Come, won't you come with me.

—Kenneth Enright
(a poem he wrote and hoped to one day have put to music)

Ken landing a Cessna 180 on a village airstrip, Kafakumba District, 1960s. Many of the villages built these small airstrips, creating a network of access that proved to be critical and lifesaving for thousands of people.

Saving lives was a critical part of being a missionary pilot. Co-founder of Wings of the Morning, a Methodist flight ministry, meant that Ken often flew desperately sick and injured people to hospitals for care. The airplanes logged millions of miles and flew thousands of emergency and medical flights. The planes were also used to deliver medicines and supplies, evacuate captives, and transport missionaries and other church workers across vast stretches of jungle and bush without roads.

Ken loved to fly and became adept at all facets of flight, including building airstrips, fixing breakdowns, flying in emergency situations, carrying every sort of passenger for many different reasons, and navigating through all types of weather.

Ken never tired of flying and considered his airplane his "home, office, and chapel."

During a furlough from Sandoa, Ken learned of the need for pilots and airplanes to support Methodist missions in Congo. He returned to Africa with a pilot's license and started the Wings of the Morning ministry with fellow missionary pilot, Paul Alexander. The men became lifesavers for staff and patients pictured here at Kapanga Methodist Hospital (now Samuteb Memorial Hospital) in southwest Congo.

The Accidents

During 30-odd years of flying, one can expect that there will be mishaps and close calls—and there were. Airplanes hit potholes on runways and broke wheel struts; engines lost power, a compass broke, a fuel line corroded. But for Ken, flying meant more than the occasional mishap. For him, it meant scary, earth-diving, cartwheeling, engine-failing, and tree smashing crashes several times. It meant injury for some, death for one, and total destruction of more than one airplane. Only son John remembered that there were seven airplane crashes in total. "It's not important," insisted the rest of the Enright family, "what is important is that he survived and continued in ministry."

Lorraine, on the other hand, was not a fan of flying. She gripped the side bar and prayed whenever they flew; she had good reason to pray. "I was with Ken in some of his crashes," she recalled. Although she disliked flying intensely and prayed the hardest when she knew her husband was in the air, she never complained. For Lorraine, flying was just another part of the job, something to be accepted as necessary to being where God wanted them to be. She remained confident in her belief that "We were always sure that we were in the right place and doing just exactly what God had for us to do."

One of the accidents occurred right in front of their little house at Lake Kafakumba. A group of five young African nursing students had gathered at the training center for a conference. The group, along with Danish missionary nurse Meta Rasmussan, climbed aboard the airplane for an hour-long flight back to their station. Meta climbed into the front seat beside Ken; the others settled into the rear seats. The plane lifted off the runway and turned out over the lake. At about 300 to 400 feet altitude, the crankshaft snapped and the engine stopped. The plane's nose turned straight down, and it plunged into the middle of Lake Kafakumba. Ken, injured and stunned but conscious, kicked out the window and swam to the surface. In horror, he realized that the nurses were all trapped in the water. He dove back into the deep water, pulling himself down to the plane's fuselage, and opened the luggage compartment. He grabbed the panicked nurses by their hair, pulling them out of the baggage opening one-by-one and pushing them up toward the surface of the water. Meta was able to climb back through the compartment on her own and exit the opening as well. The nurses all made it to the surface where they gulped life-giving air. People on shore had seen the plane go down and immediately dispatched canoes to the rescue.

The cause of the accident was determined to be a cracked crankshaft in the engine that had just been purchased in Nairobi for the airplane. When it snapped, the plane went into a perpendicular dive. It was very unusual, indeed miraculous, that everybody lived. If not for Ken's quick thinking and extraordinary swimming skills, it is doubtful that everyone would have been saved from the submerged plane. Some think it gave the crocodiles in the area a good scare, too.

Two particular accidents, however, caused Ken and Lorraine great injury. The first (in 1962 or 1963) happened at Sakaji, at the Plymouth Brethren School in Zambia, which many missionary children attended, including the Enright children. On this particular day, Ken and Lorraine flew to Sakaji to pick up their children for Christmas break (three of them were at Sakaji at the time: John, Elaine, and Eileen). They landed without incident, settled the children in the back seat for the flight home, and Lorraine climbed in beside Ken, carrying the cake she was taking back with them for Christmas. The sunny day had turned rainy, softening the dirt runway, and winds had picked up among the trees lining the air strip. Three airplanes took off just before them. But when Ken attempted to take off, the smaller Cessna 170 B he was piloting was simply underpowered for the soft runway and the blowing winds. The plane could not get airborne as the wind pushed it downward, crashing and turning over as it fell to the ground.

Another missionary couple, Dr. Glenn and Lena Eschtruth, were also at Sakaji that day. (They were stationed at

Kapanga Hospital.) Lena remembered running to the plane to help get the family out. She ordered someone to get her physician–husband as she watched Lorraine being lifted from the plane. "She had face lacerations and many broken bones," Lena recalled, "including six broken in her foot and arm." Lorraine was taken to the tiny Brethren hospital where Dr. Glenn stitched up her face. He found very tiny suture thread and stitched so carefully that she never showed any scarring from his stitches. "It was really a miracle," Lorraine insisted as she remembered the deep slash across her forehead and over her eye.

Lena watched the children for a short time, and then they stayed with local missionaries while Ken and Lorraine were hospitalized in Kitwe, Zambia. The two were released from the hospital, but ended up staying in a local hotel because the Methodist Guest House was full for the Christmas holiday. Lorraine returned to the hospital to have surgery on a foot, including the placement of steel wires to hold her toes straight. Finally, the family was flown back to Congo, spending Christmas Eve with missionaries at Kasaji and having Christmas dinner with other missionaries at their home station of Sandoa. "That year we didn't wrap our gifts or have cake," remembered Lorraine.

Later Lorraine had to travel to Kapanga Hospital to have Dr. Glenn remove the wires from her toes. She remembered two things about that trip: the difficulty Dr. Glenn had in locating and removing the wires from her toes and foot—"The bottom of my foot looked like hamburger as he shot in Novocain, then cut and searched for all the wires," she said. The other memory was of the 18 roadblocks they went through on their drive to Kapanga. No fuss was made of the whole matter, however. The children had been unhurt and returned to school after Christmas break; Ken and Lorraine healed from their injuries and went back to work. Both continued to fly.

Another flight, the last that Ken flew, ended tragically. Both Ken and Lorraine suffered painful, crushing injuries; another passenger was killed and a fourth walked away unhurt. The four lifted into the blue equatorial sky that day with Ken at the controls, a Congolese friend Mbuyu (who was also the family cook) sat in front with him, Lorraine sat behind on the right side, and a Methodist district superintendent sat to her left behind Ken. The group was flying to Lake Kafakumba but was making a short stop-over at another Methodist mission station at Luena. As the plane approached its first destination, a sound, a sensation, perhaps a premonition, prompted Lorraine to lean forward and ask Ken if they were going to crash. "Yes," he answered, just before the plane tumbled from the sky. It hit trees and slammed into a large ant hill at high speed before smashing across the ground. The airplane was far short of the runway and broke into pieces as it crumpled and shattered across the long grass.

Another missionary pilot, Tom Wolford, was also preparing to land at Luena and had received no reply from Ken as he tried to make radio contact. When Tom landed, he heard people shouting about an airplane crash. He raced to his car, grabbed his first-aid bag and drove through the tall grass to the scene. He and several Congolese pastors and friends began cutting the passengers out of the twisted wreckage. Tom's training as an emergency medical technician and the supplies in his medical bag saved Lorraine from bleeding to death that day.

Sadly, Mbuyu died in the crash. The district superintendent walked away without injury. Ken and Lorraine were hurt badly and taken to Luena Hospital to be stabilized. Tom returned to his airplane and flew to the Methodist mission hospital at Matwaba to pick up Dr. Ray Williams and bring him back to help. Missionary nurses, Lena Eschtruth (serving at Manono at the time) and Jeri Allen (at Kapanga Methodist Hospital) were flown in to Luena to help nurse the pair. After two critical days in the local hospital, Ken and Lorraine were taken to John and Kendra's house while they awaited medical evacuation. Because John and Kendra were in the United States at the time, their house became a hospital, with their king-sized bed being used to try to keep their parents stable. Jeri worked on Ken; Lena worked on Lorraine. Both had life-threatening injuries. The entire muscle of Lorraine's leg from knee to ankle had been almost completely sliced off. She developed a bacterial infection, while dirt and grass and straw continued to embed her flesh.

With only Tylenol to dull their patients' pain, the nurses kept a round-the-clock vigil. Several days passed while they waited for paperwork to be approved to fly the Enrights back to the United States. Lena remembered two funny instances from the days in Luena. "You know, you had to laugh sometimes," she said. The first time she went to the medicine closet to find some Tylenol, she was startled when she reached in for the medicine and a snake fell onto her arm—a rubber snake, that is, which had been placed there as a joke by one of John and Kendra's sons. Another laugh came in the middle of a night when Lena climbed up on the huge bed and position herself between Ken and Lorraine so that she could pull Lorraine back up into a better sleeping position. In the darkness she heard Ken chuckle, "Well, Lena, I never expected you to come between us." The group stayed at John and Kendra's house in Luena for about a week, keeping Ken and Lorraine stable and waiting for the red tape of an African air bureaucracy to clear.

With paperwork secured, Tom Wolford piloted the mission's Aero Commander out of Luena with Ken and Lorraine on stretchers on the floor and Lena and Jerri attending them. The plane flew to Lubumbashi, the region's commercial center, where they were transferred onto another plane headed for the country's capital of Kinshasa. Maneuvering the stretchers around the sharp corner into the plane's cabin was very difficult and caused Lorraine wrenching, twisting pain. At Kinshasa, Lena and Jeri gasped as they watched a team carry Ken's stretcher down the stairway of the plane. "Ken was a big and heavy man," said Lena, "and the group could barely handle the stretcher. The stretcher slanted so badly going down the steps that I thought they were going to lose him. It was just so awful." Then Lorraine had to be wrenched around the plane's sharp interior corner again. The group boarded Sabena Airlines (their flight from

Kinshasa to Brussels) and was greeted in Brussels by people driving a garbage truck with a hydraulic lift. The lift was a godsend and made transferring Ken and Lorraine much less painful and precarious.

Family and medical staff gathered at the Atlanta airport to await their arrival. The Methodist mission board sent their Medical Mission Director, Dr. Devon Corbitt to meet them at the airport. Dr. Corbitt had been a doctor in Congo in years past, and had delivered Elinda at the Kapanga Hospital. The Board hired an air ambulance for the last leg of the journey to Daytona Beach, where they were met by son-in-law and physician, Dick Fisher, and his hand-chosen team of doctors. They were hospitalized near to family and the skilled care needed for extended recovery. Lorraine begged her doctor not to send Ken home ahead of her, and he didn't. Later, the two went home together, with everyone marveling at their unfolding recoveries.

Ken described the accident in a letter to friends several months later:

> It's been four months since that fateful day when we came tumbling out of the sky. A concussion has erased all that from my mind, and I came to about 40 minutes later, lying in a field after they had cut me out of the wreck. I heard my wife praying, and learned of my friend's death, and then passed out again. The next few days are a blur, and I only remember a sea of PAIN and the vast comfort of African friends and missionaries as they ministered to Lorraine and I.

Ken's injuries were life-threatening: a broken sternum and a chest compression that collapsed a lung; ribs broken off his breastbone and a spinal compression from fractures in his spinal column (all of which made breathing extremely painful); a concussion, acid burns, cuts, and internal injuries. The severity and pain of his injuries, let alone the blurred and tortured thinking of brain injury, brought him to one of the lowest places in his life. He wanted to give up. Unable to move and enduring unspeakable pain, he later insisted that it was only "a Loving Lord Jesus and praying friends that brought us through."

If Ken was hurt badly, Lorraine's list of injuries was even longer. Everything, it seemed, was broken, strained, bruised, burned, or cut. Horrific injuries and gaping wounds threatened her life. The injury of most concern, though, was the massive leg wound and the bleeding and bacterial infection that had set in. Nurses had to literally hold the muscle of her leg on at times.

Friends and family left nothing to chance as they gathered that day at the Atlanta airport. Lorraine still smiles as she recalled how family had planned to fulfill the requirement of a physician meeting the airplane in Atlanta—just in case the Mission Board didn't get a doctor there in time. They commissioned CPA son-in-law (Eileen's husband), John Ledgerwood, to play the role of a physician if needed to expedite their parents' transport. Lorraine chuckled as she recalled hearing an overhead announcement from airport speakers, "Calling Dr. Ledgerwood. Calling Dr. Ledgerwood." Fortunately, John's medical skills were never necessary.

For many months Ken and Lorraine endured treatment after treatment, sometimes picking and scraping the continual emergence of grass and glass through their wounds. Their recoveries were cause for praise, and both their doctors would admit that "We only treat patients…God heals them." Lorraine continues to carry fierce scars from her injuries. Much of the muscle and skin of one leg were torn off, leaving her calf misshapen and shrunken. Although plastic surgery and skin grafts could have made the leg look better, Lorraine thought better of the treatment. "You can't really see it that much from the front," she insisted, and so she did not have the surgery. Fortunately, long pants and longish skirts help cover the tightened, twisted skin. From the side, though, it is a reminder of God's amazing grace.

Perhaps the two recovered faster than normal because they were looking forward to their daughter Elinda Beth's wedding to

Nate Steury. Elinda remembered her mother insisting that she would "walk down that aisle, no matter what." Sure enough, there was still glass working itself out of her leg, but Lorraine walked down the aisle. "She's a tough one," admitted Elinda.

After several months of treatment in America, Ken and Lorraine returned to their work in the Kafakumba district and at Manono. They considered their near-death injuries and the pain of suffering as helpful in their work. Their miraculous survival perhaps fueled their final years of full-time ministry and the intensity of the hardest years they'd ever known. They never forgot that theirs were the first two lives saved by a container of medical supplies sent from friends back home and that a very wide circle of friends loved them back to health with "untold prayers, cards, flowers, telephone calls, gifts, and every conceivable expression of love and support."

Ken and Lorraine's response to the airplane accidents, especially those that involved injury, even death, was a testament to their faith and perseverance. Ken showed a remarkable lack of fear as a bush pilot. He climbed back into the airplane many times after harrowing experiences with violent soldiers, uncooperative officials, threatening weather, mechanical problems, dangerous airstrips, and multiple crashes. He loved the ministry of flying—whether carrying sick and injured people for medical help, flying to remote places to preach or hold revivals, or transporting pastors and church leaders on necessary church business.

Lorraine, although she disliked flying and was always concerned for Ken when he was in the air, never complained. She, too, had a remarkable ability to put fear behind her and move forward with what was needed to carry on their ministries. "God blessed her with the ability to close one door and keep on going," remarked Elinda. "She never lived in the past, even though there were some really horrible situations. She looked back—and she always had a good memory for what was positive in a situation—but she really chose to look at the glass as half full," Elinda continued. Lorraine's ability to move past almost impossible situations was a strength that enabled her and Ken to stay in the field in Congo for a lifetime. "She had to be that way or she would have cracked. A lot of other wives did crack, and the husbands packed the family up and they came back to the States feeling as if they had unfinished business. My mother is emotionally drawn to the positive, and that is a gift," Elinda smiled.

Endnotes

(1) Wings of the Morning continues as an aviation ministry of the United Methodist Church in Congo. It provides transportation for medical emergencies, supplies, visiting educators, teams, leaders, and other church needs in the region. More information is available at www.umcmissions.org.

(2) Read more about the life, ministry, and death of Burleigh Law at the hand of Simba soldiers in the book, *Appointment Congo*, written by his widow, Virginia Law Shell. The book is available by writing to Appointment Congo, P.O. Box 98764, Raleigh, NC 27624.

During the Simba Rebellion, missionaries were captured at the Methodist station of Wembo Nyama in 1964 as part of the uprising of Simba rebels in Central and Eastern Congo. Wembo Nyama was located north and east of Katanga, where Ken and Lorraine were stationed, and was surrounded by equatorial forests in contrast to the vast grasslands of the Katanga Plateau. The Simba were known for the brutality with which they executed those they considered enemies: thousands of Congolese fell victim to the Simba, including government officials, political leaders of opposition parties, provincial and local police, school teachers, and others they believed to be Westernized. (Interested readers can learn more about the cruelty of the Simba toward Westerners by researching the Stanleyville Massacre. The event ended 111 days of captivity when rebels gathered hostages into the city's center and opened fire indiscriminately into the crowd, killing fifty, even as Belgian paratroopers entered the city.)

When the missionaries were taken captive by Simba rebels at Wembo Nyama, then, they were in the hands of cruel and unpredictable captors. The missionary community prayed fervently for their release. Fellow missionary, Burleigh Law, was murdered in the 1964 uprising. The rescue of the women held captive at Wembo was a momentous occasion. The flight of Ken Enright and Don Watts to the station was fraught with danger and unpredictability, especially so for Ken who was flying into unknown territory without familiar markers, running low on fuel, and forced to negotiate with rebels at the airfield. The successful evacuation of the women was a certain answer to prayer for many around the world.

(3)   Flying and flight-following were such an integral part of mission life in Southern Congo that missionaries forever remembered not only the names of the places at which they lived, but also the numbers assigned to them by Wings of the Morning. Although the numbers mean little to others, they were lifesaving for those who served. Following is a list of the Katanga mission stations with the numbers that identified them for radio networking:

20	Mulungwishi
21	Kafakumba
22	Sandoa
23	Kapanga
24	Kamina
39	Lubumbashi
40	Likasi
41	Kolwezi
55	Lodja
56	Wembo Nyama
74	Kasaji
83	Kinshasa
99	Kananga

CHAPTER 11

Kafakumba Pastors' School: The move to Zambia, 1999

"If anyone is in Christ, he is a new creation; the old has gone, the new has come! All this is from God, who reconciled us to himself through Christ."
—2 Corinthians 5:17-18a

The political situation in Congo remained unstable from the time of its Independence in 1960. Varied rebel and militia groups continued their attempts to overthrow the government, outside armies invaded across Congo's long borders, and daily life carried continual threats of violence and destruction. Kafakumba Pastors' School was always held after roads had dried from the rainy season's downpours, and travel became possible again. By the early 1990s, however, it wasn't the roads that made travel difficult, but on-going war.

It finally became impossible for students to travel to Lake Kafakumba and for supplies to be brought in. Instructors could no longer travel to the site, and basic necessities to run the school became impossible to obtain. Finally, in late 1998, Ken and Lorraine faced the reality of having to leave Lake Kafakumba for good. They had no choice but to leave their beloved home, many friends, and the ministries they loved, especially Pastors' School. A fellow Wings of the Morning pilot flew them out—a story told in another chapter—and they joined John and Kendra in the United States. (John and Kendra had also evacuated, spending much of 1998 on medical leave.)

Assigned to North Katanga (called North Shaba during the years of President Mobutu Sese Seko), John continued to hope for enough peace and stability to return to work there. But his father had another idea: move Pastors' School to Zambia! It seemed such a brilliant idea: Zambia was a peaceful country, it had a long history of Methodist missionary presence, and it had a history of collaborating with churches in Congo. The Copper Belt country along its northern border had a strong Congolese presence and was central to pastors travelling between Congo, Zambia, Tanzania, and other central African countries. The region had much better roads, and either Kitwe or Ndola (two large cities on the border) could supply all they needed to restart the school. Ken plunged headlong into his plan to recreate the campus they'd left behind at Lake Kafakumba.

Initially, John continued his plan to return to Congo, the place to which he believed he was called for a lifetime. He remained open, however, and agreed to travel to Zambia with Ken in early 1999 to explore the idea. The men met with missionaries and church leaders in Ndola. They became reacquainted with Congolese they had known before who had immigrated across the border into Zambia. In a providential moment, they met John Kayeye, an architect and construction engineer they had known in Congo, and the idea of a new campus in Zambia began to take hold in John's mind.

In what John can only describe as "miraculous," he found a site perfectly suited to building a training center. Located on a main highway just a few miles from the city of Ndola, the land was for sale by the Yugoslavian trucking company that had developed it. The property had a large, rambling building that was well-suited for remodeling into offices and living space. It had space for classrooms and a large lot perfect for dormitories, an auditorium, classrooms for the women and children's programs, and dorms for visitors. Several homes were already built along the property's edge—perfect for staff—with plenty of room for more. There was enough land for a soccer field for youth programs and fields for planting; for a holding pond for dry-season irrigation; and space on which to develop the businesses that would become central to Kafakumba's model of community development. There was also a well for fresh water.

The area's effect on John was immediate and life-changing. He quickly envisioned the potential for ministry, not only rebuilding Kafakumba Pastors' School, but a full-blown vision of ministries that could totally transform the region. In his mind, he saw the ministry as if it were already completed: a training center open for anyone to use, the emergence of Pastors' School, women's seminars, churches meeting the spiritual and physical needs of their communities, ministries of health and education for all, clean water, proper housing, businesses, and lively commerce. It is not an exaggeration that John envisioned a slice of heaven on earth for one of the poorest places on the planet. The property had potential, but it still needed an enormous amount of work. John and Ken went ahead and purchased the land and returned to share the dream with their wives back in the United States.

Until 1999, Kafakumba Pastors' School was held each year without interruption. It was an amazing accomplishment considering the destruction and violence of the wars that had plagued the entire Katanga Province and whole of Congo. The fact that the school only missed classes one year as the Enright families faced evacuation, illness, immigration, and building an entirely new campus in a new country, was probably an even greater feat. In 1999, Ken and Lorraine, along with John and Kendra and their sons, moved to a community near Ndola to establish the Kafakumba Training Center at the site of the former trucking company. John and Kendra lived there permanently; Ken and Lorraine divided their time between Florida and Africa, this time in Zambia and not Congo.

John and Ken picked up their habit of preaching in nearby villages and in the city. Soon several new congregations emerged; buildings were purchased for these churches, and a United Methodist presence grew stronger in the Zambian Copperbelt. Other missionaries who had evacuated from Congo also moved to the region, and the Methodist church structure linked these ministries with those of Southern Congo. The United Methodist Bishop of Southern Congo, Kainda Katembo, welcomed the missionaries and ministries of Kafakumba to the region and remained a strong supporter. He assigned his assistant to help direct the new Training Center and created a strong bond between his office and the work at Kafakumba. Several fellow missionary families joined John and Kendra full-time at the Kafakumba Training Center, helping support emerging churches, pastor training, women's programs, education, and community development.

With only the one-year absence, Kafakumba Pastors' School resumed classes in 2000. More than 100 students came to the site from Congo, Tanzania, Zambia, and Senegal. Class sizes had been about 120 students in Congo, and the number remained about the same at the Zambia campus. Because the wives and children came with their student husbands after the fourth year, the number grew with the addition of about 50 wives and 90 children. (Notably, a growing number of women have been entering ministry, so it is not uncommon for the pastor-in-training to be a woman.)

New buildings began to rise on the site. John Kayeye designed and built a beautiful auditorium in the center of the property, and dormitories replaced the tiny brick student houses of the Congo campus. Oil-covered dirt and concrete gave way to attractive landscaping and walkways. Simple classrooms were created, and a section of one building became a large dining room, although cooking still took place outside or over charcoal-filled braziers on the floor. Students were no longer able to bring their own food supplies over the long distances, so meals were cooked and provided on-site for everyone. For many, this meant enjoying a full stomach for the first time in their lives. Almost every man, woman, and child gained weight during Pastors' School.

Classes resumed as they had been when held at Lake Kafakumba, and the name of the school remained the same. Many of the same teachers continued to teach, and the subjects remained almost identical. One subject area, however, took on added importance in Zambia: community development—or at minimum developing practical commerce that allowed pastors to return to villages and become entrepreneurs. Providing basic training in community development and the thinking skills needed to start and maintain simple businesses has been integral to the Kafakumba model of pastor training. The practical application of life skills has become as important as the theological training that Pastors' School provides. Technology has arrived in the classroom, too. Preaching classes include taping, replaying, and analyzing sermons. A computer lab introduces pastors to the wonders of the Internet and electronic communication. Although many live in villages without electricity in homes, it is not uncommon for cafes or bars to have electricity and for villagers to have access to television or the Internet there. (Just as cell phones have become commonplace in regions without access to land lines, technology will continue to change village life in remote places.)

Kafakumba Pastors' School has always included Congolese leadership in its development. Although Ken started the School, it has been nurtured and supported by African bishops and leaders within African churches. Beginning in the late 1970s, young pastor Kasongo Munza began to teach at Pastors' School. (Kasongo had been part of Ken and Lorraine's *Kipendano* river boat ministry and evangelization crusades during the years they were stationed at Manono.) He was very involved in teaching and behind-the-scenes logistics at Pastors' School, all the while pastoring a church or working at Mulungwishi Seminary. When the Kafakumba Training Center was being built in Zambia and Pastors' School was moved to that location, he moved to Zambia and continued as Director of the School. (1) When Kasongo became ill in 2001, another Congolese minister involved in Pastors' School, Pastor Tanga, became a co-director with him. He remains one of the ministers in Congo's largest Methodist church, the Jerusalem Church in Lubumbashi, and a primary resource for the school in that country. Pastor Robert Kilembo, a Congolese transplant to Zambia and graduate of Mulungwishi Seminary, joined the Kafakumba Training Center staff and assumed leadership of the Training Center, as well as worked as the assistant to Bishop Katembo. Each year, the Reverends Kilembo and Tanga sit together with other leaders of the Kafakumba Training Center to plan the school's courses, teachers, and logistics. It never was—and never will be—a small feat to train leaders. African villages, filled with the old traditions of fetishes, sorcery, and deceptions of Animist worldviews, require nothing less than the Spirit of God lived out in the extraordinary lives of Christians. Those who teach, and those who learn, at Kafakumba have always been linked in a powerful understanding of God at work in the world.

In 2005, Pastors' School was reintroduced in the Democratic Republic of the Congo. Classes were held at both the Zambia campus as well as a Congo location. Logistics had always been difficult for Pastors' School in Congo in the past, and had finally become impossible to overcome. However, continuing to bring students from Congo to Zambia was also difficult, especially with the high cost of visas, transportation, and food. The School has been held in varied locations in Congo in recent years (most recently at Mulungwishi Seminary) and the goal remains to continue holding pastor training in both countries. The growing number of clergy from Methodist and other denominations in Central Africa rely on the school for their training. The folks back at home in the villages are relying on it too.

It is one thing to talk about Kafakumba Pastors' School as an idea or in terms of its location, curriculum or structure. For the Enright family, the School is a passion, and it is very personal. All family members remain involved in some means of support for the ministries their parents started. "When you say 'Kafakumba,' I think of people—individuals, friends, villages, pastors effectively ministering to the villagers," remarked Kenny one day. He shared a memory from a time in his adolescence. He was hunting about 60 miles from home in a very sparsely populated part of Sandoa Territory when he entered a village. To his surprise, he found family friend Silas Mwamba preaching to the villagers under a mango tree. It was mid-week, and rather than disturb the congregation, he and his hunting comrades sat alongside a hut and watched. The service continued and the hunters remained unnoticed by Silas, whose back was to them. Kenny remembered thinking how odd it was that this older man had ridden his bicycle 30 miles on a weekday to preach to the members of this small and obscure village. The memory made a profound impression on Kenny; he still finds the pastor's dedication and the desire and need of the people for the message remarkable.

Kenny has remained a friend of many in Congo over the years. He firmly believes that village pastors, like those trained at Kafakumba, are the best hope for Christianity in Africa, and perhaps in the world. As the Church continues to grow exponentially in the Global South (especially in Africa), and decline in the West, he views the development of pastors for those churches as a critical job of Christianity. "They are simply the hope of the Church," he emphasized. "My parent's investment in Africa is already paying off for all of us. Just look at the number of churches in central Africa and how they have already affected some of the denominations of the West (the Methodist and Episcopal churches, for example). My parents sacrifice is a small part of a much larger picture."

The story of the villagers of Mwinbez, told in Chapter four, is a powerful story about partnerships. The people of the village welcomed Ken and Lorraine as friends and fellow believers in Christ. They started a church and did their part in building a place of worship. All was in place except for a pastor, at which point the village elders became desperate and built the roadblock. Ken was not allowed to pass through the block until he had promised to provide a pastor for the group—which he did. The villagers were not only friends to Ken and Lorraine, but showed great courage in protecting their lives during varied rebel attacks, including during their captivity in Kolwezi. The whole business of partnering with people, building churches, providing pastoral leadership, and continuing the relationships of believers across different cultures all played out in Mwinbez. The issues of church growth and pastor training are an ever-present need in Central Africa. It is serious business and of paramount value to Christianity and the worldwide Church. (2)

Another Enright connection

"This is Jesus' work. It is the front line of ministry," remarked Nate Steury, long-time Pastors' School teacher. Nate (the son of famed missionary doctor and founder of Tenwick Hospital in Kenya, Dr. Ernie Steury) went to school with and later married Elinda Enright. A pilot and accountant before attending seminary, Nate became a United Methodist minister in Florida, where he has pastored for many years. In 2000, however, he began traveling to Africa to teach in Pastors' School each year.

"Kafakumba Pastors' School is a beautiful community where amazing friendships are made. My favorite thing is meeting the local village pastors. These are guys who live in huts, often without an education past the fourth or sixth grade; they might have one book and it's a Bible. But they care for people," he continued. These village pastors receive minimal salaries from their congregations, sometimes little more than gifts of food (such as peanuts or corn)—gifts from people who bring what they can. The pastors suffer the ravages of poverty and disease along with everybody else in their communities, but keep going on faith. Nate has been moved by his role in touching lives at

Pastors' School. "These men and women return to hundreds of villages and touch other lives," he continued.

Because of their minister's involvement at Kafakumba, Florida's Melbourne United Methodist Church has supported Pastors' School in several ways. They have provided each freshman pastor with a Bible in his or her native language and a bicycle. Eight years later, each graduate receives an *African Bible Commentary* (a one-volume resource by African scholars) and $100, which provides enough capital for the family to start a small business to support them (purchasing chickens, bees and hives, etc.). "We've tried to focus our gifts as an investment in their beginning," said Nate. The church is looking at solar-powered Kindles to replace the Bible commentary.

Elinda, too, has retained a deep passion for the people of Central Africa and the school her parents loved. As a nurse, she recognizes the important role of good health, while also recognizing the very destructive role of poverty on individual and community lives. Malaria and many other preventable diseases bring significant sorrow to village life. Like her mother, Elinda recognizes the critical role of women to the health and well-being of their families and communities. As a doctoral student in nurse administration, Elinda has been working to forge bonds between health providers in Zambia and the University of Central Florida.

For both Nate and Elinda, this passion for Kafakumba Pastors' School and for the people of the region has bloomed into a commitment to move to Zambia to work full-time. As of this writing, they are making plans for the move, which should take place in mid-2013. Nate will provide leadership at the Pastors' School, working with its current director, Pastor Robert Kilembo, and others. Elinda will provide leadership in a healthcare partnership that will benefit both those in medical training in Zambia as well as in Florida.

Yes, the prayers of Esther Farrier have had a far-reaching effect. Prayers for her daughter, Lorraine, and for her future son-in-law, Ken, brought together a powerful pair in ministry. Prayers for their faithfulness and fruitfulness in ministry were answered fully. Prayers for her grandchildren have been answered; all of them retain strong connections to Africa and continue to support Kafakumba ministries, manifested most particularly in the lives of John and Kendra Enright and Elinda and Nate Steury. Esther and many others have prayed in the past. Churches, individuals, and other groups continue a widening circle of prayer and support. There is no doubt that the many ministries of Kafakumba, especially the Pastors' School, are the answers to many prayers. Especially those rising up from the villages of Central Africa.

Endnote

1. Kasongo Munza authored a book titled, *A Letter to Africa about Africa*, Kafakumba Training Center, Google books, 2005.
2. Two books have been especially helpful in understanding the shift of Christianity's center from the West to the Global South, most specifically to Africa. They are *The Next Christendom: The Coming of Global Christianity* and *The New Faces of Christianity: Believing the Bible in the Global South*. Both are authored by Philip Jenkins, Distinguished Professor of History and Religious Studies at Pennsylvania State University.

A recent class of graduates from the Kafakumba Pastors' School in Zambia. The group includes attendees from Congo, Zambia, and Tanzania. A growing number of women are joining the ranks of pastors in the quickly growing United Methodist churches in the region.

Bicycles make all the difference in the world for village pastors, who use them as their primary means of transportation. Pastors routinely travel many hours, even days, on their bikes to reach churches in remote villages. A bicycle is given to every first-year student at Kafakumba Pastors' School, a gift from Methodists in the United States who value their importance to ministry.

Pastors receive a copy of the classic *Egermeier Bible Story Book* in Swahili when they attend Pastors' School. The book was translated and printed with memorial funds given at the time of Ken's death. For many village pastors, the Bible and this book are their only printed resources.

The Worship Center is the focus of activity at the Kafakumba Training Center, Zambia. Here, a group gathers at Pastors' School; others book the Center for conferences during the ten months when Pastors' School is not in session. A Women's Center, Children's Center and playground, dormitories, classrooms, homes, offices, dining hall, sports field, farm ground, and work buildings are also located at the main campus.

The Kafakumba Training Center was founded in Zambia in 1999 as home to the relocated Kafakumba Pastors' School. Continuing war forced missionaries from Congo, making it impossible to continue the school at its original location at Lake Kafakumba. The new site near Ndola, Zambia, is very close to Congo's southern border, and Zambia's peaceful history makes it a good location for serving churches in Central Africa. The Kafakumba Training Center is booked year-round for training, camps, conferences, and seminars; it is also the center of a growing United Methodist presence in Zambia.

Women gather regularly for fellowship, study, crafts, and entrepreneurship classes through-out the year at the Training Center. In addition, women are a regular part of the six-week Pastors' School, and a Womens' Empowerment Seminar is a popular leadership conference held annually at the Center.

Kafakumba Training Center, Zambia, includes a commercial woodshop where doors, win-dows, flooring, and furniture are crafted. Other businesses, such as raising bananas, aloe, fish, and honey provide jobs while also providing funds for the Center.

Bananas have been lifesavers for many women, enabling them to earn money to send children to school and put food on the table. Bananas planted at the Kafakumba Training Center in Zambia are sold at minimal cost to local women, who then take them to markets to sell. The laughter of the women at the banana depot each morning is the sound of hope.

Pastor Robert Kilembo is the director of Pastors' School as well as the Bishop's assistant in the region. He is a vital link between the Training Center and the many United Methodist congregations in the region. Originally from Congo, he and his family make their home at Kafakumba in Zambia.

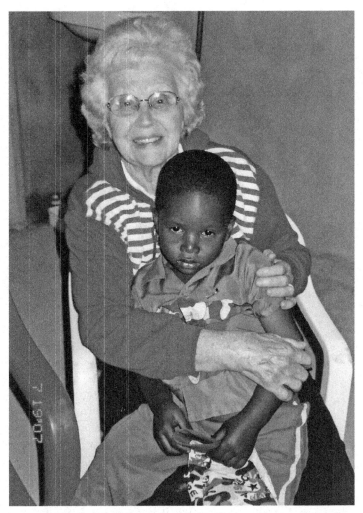

Lorraine continues to live in Zambia part of each year, working with children during Pastors' School and overseeing the hundreds of children in the God's Kids clubs. She is never too busy to spend a little time with a child in need.

CHAPTER 12

Into the Future: The author speaks

"There has never been the slightest doubt in my mind that the God who started this great work in you would keep at it and bring it to a flourishing finish on the very day Christ Jesus appears."

—Philippians 1:6 (The Message)

A remarkable shift is occurring in the history of the Christian church. And Ken and Lorraine found themselves in the forefront of that change in terms of both place and time. Central Africa proved to be very open to Christianity, and Post-World War II missionaries found themselves welcome in the region.

Churches in Europe and North America had not yet felt the ground shifting, but within decades the shift has become unmistakable. During the 50+ years that Ken and Lorraine spent in Africa, the geographic and demographic centers of Christianity were moving with them. Religion scholar Philip Jenkins insists that this emerging global Christianity is growing as a grassroots movement. (1) Continued growth in Africa and Asia certainly support that idea. While many churches continue to decline in numbers and attendance in Europe and the United

States, African churches are growing quickly. In sheer numbers, the United States is predicted to remain overwhelmingly Christian, but explosive population growth around the world points toward large growth of Christianity in the Majority World, or Global South. "Amazing as it may appear to a blasé West, Christianity exercises an overwhelming global appeal, which shows not the slightest sign of waning," says Jenkins.

Ken and Lorraine may not have known the statistics of church growth, but they lived with this growth every day during their years in Congo. Ken preached to huge crowds. He oversaw the building of hundreds of churches. He trained hundreds of pastors and worked alongside a growing number of talented and dedicated African leaders. Lorraine, too, found herself totally immersed in the needs of teachers and pastors' wives, as well as needed ministries with women and children. Because the ravages of poverty tore at their hearts, they dedicated enormous amounts of time to ministries of healing, food, and clean water. They were thoroughly Wesleyan, that is, they followed the teachings of John Wesley to live out a practical and holistic gospel that tended to both body and soul.

Ken and Lorraine may have been too busy to notice, but their own Methodist denomination was also changing. Their time at Mulungwishi, the Methodist center for education in Congo, convinced them that the higher education available at the site was inadequate to meet the region's needs. Subsequent years in the rural communities of Sandoa and Kafakumba confirmed their belief that their biggest effect could be had by devoting themselves to the needs of rural pastors. Urban assignments to Lubumbashi, Kolwezi, and Manono—always in conjunction with assignments to the Kafakumba area—taught them of the unique needs of urban centers, including its grinding poverty. And in the middle of this, Methodism was becoming a very large denomination in Congo, second only to the Catholic Church in numbers.

Today, the two conferences of the United Methodist Church in Congo's Katanga Province are the fastest growing in its worldwide connection. (Ken and Lorraine lived all their years in Africa in those conferences.) The African presence at the denomination's quadrennial General Conference has become very pronounced. Because the General Conference is the only body that speaks officially for the United Methodist Church, the votes of African delegates are having an increasing influence on church policies. Voices from the African church are being heard throughout the denomination. Indeed, the voices of African believers are being heard throughout the Church worldwide.

Ah, but here's the rub: Churches are growing, but the need for pastor training is not keeping up with the need. Ken knew this in 1963. He and other missionaries and African church leaders could not keep up with the need for training. With limited university educations available for some, Ken and Lorraine turned their eyes toward the greatest need: village churches, village pastors. (2) That need has only grown in the 50 years since those first classes were held on the shore of Lake Kafakumba.

Kafakumba Pastors' School marks its 50-year anniversary in 2013. Fifty years is a remarkable anniversary for a ministry birthed in hope but raised in a country gutted by poverty and war. It has succeeded because of the remarkable partnerships of people who believe in churches and those who lead them. The life and ministry of Jesus Christ is based on the idea of a Kingdom, a community of love and faith that transforms the world around it. Partners with Kafakumba believe that God's love is transformative, it changes the status quo. It changes people. It heals brokenness and feeds hunger. It replaces hatred with love and conflict with peace.

Kafakumba Pastors' School and the ministries associated with it are based on this understanding of the Gospel. Its core values include these seven beliefs:

- Community: Living with respect for neighbors and the world we share.
- Servanthood: Following Christ's example of service to others.

- Focusing on the least: Committing to the poor and those living at the margins.
- Trusteeship: Believing that all we have is a gift, to be cared for and entrusted to the future.
- Nonviolence: Living as peacemakers, especially recognizing the devastation inflicted on war's innocent victims.
- Love: Committing to love God and neighbor as Christ instructed; making compassionate love the guide for all endeavors.
- Unity: Seeking the unity and sacredness of life, work, and the world around us.

The future of Kafakumba Pastors' School relies on continuing partnerships. This model for training village pastors has proven to be very effective, and the need for it continues to grow. Jenkins writes that the Christian population of Congo is expected to increase from 34 million in 2000 to 70 million in 2025 and to 121 million in 2050.

The need for support continues even as huge strides are being made in community development and sustainability at the Kafakumba Training Center. Kafakumba's long-term goal is to be completely self-supporting, but the needs have been too great for that to happen. The African church is alive in faith, but it remains impoverished and unable yet to pay the costs of training its leadership.

A major step was taken in 2011 when the Kafakumba Pastors' School Fund was established, a foundation to provide the Pastors' School with a perpetual funding source. With the future of the Pastors' School secured, other ministries will be strengthened—ministries of mercy and compassion that heal, feed, clothe, educate, empower, and encourage people in need of hope.

There is still a lot of work to do! We all have a chance to step into the flow of history and make a difference—especially in places where we see God already at work in powerful ways.

Ken and Lorraine Enright stepped forward with their lives. Others have stepped forward with gifts of prayer, presence, time, talents, and money. Here is a place where some of the world's great needs might, indeed, meet our deep gladness….and create a place blessed by God's presence.

Get Connected

Go to the website: www.kafakumba.org to learn about the wide-ranging ministries at the Kafakumba Training Center, including its premier program, Kafakumba Pastors' School. Another website, www.liftingafrica.org details the for-profit, community development organization related to the Training Center.

- Donations for the ongoing support of the Training Center or Pastors' School: Checks should be made out to the Kafakumba Development Projects Fund and mailed to Kafakumba Development Projects Fund, 5833 State Road 132, Pendleton, IN 46064. All donations are 100% tax deductible in the U.S., and donors will be provided a tax receipt.
- Donations to the Foundation, which will provide a perpetual funding source for Kafakumba Pastors' School: Checks should be made out to The Kafakumba Pastors' School Single Charity Fund (please write "Reference Fund #971073" on the memo line). Send your check to: National Christian Foundation, 70 East 91st Street, Suite 101, Indianapolis, IN 46240.
- For United Methodist churches and individuals who want to give to Kafakumba through the church's Advance mission program can do so in one of three ways. First, checks can be placed in your church's offering plate with instructions that it be given to Kafakumba Pastors' School and Scholarships, Advance

Projects #11438. The church will send your gift on through denominational channels. Second, donate by credit card by calling 888-252-6174. Third, by mail: Make checks payable to ADVANCE GCFA, writing Kafakumba Pastors' School, Advance #11438 on the memo line of the check. Send check to: Advance GCFA, PO Box 9068, New York, NY 10087-9068.

- Sign up for e-newsletters from Kafakumba missionaries—and read them—on the website at www.kafakumba.org.
- Get involved. Schedule a speaker. Pray. Connect your church. Write. The website includes contact information, email addresses, and related links: www.kafakumba.org.

"Together we can equip African people with a better understanding of the principles of the Kingdom of God in order to transform their lives. This is your time! Please get involved!"

—Pastor Robert Kilembo, Ndola, Zambia

John and Kendra Enright continue to oversee the work at the Kafakumba Training Center. John's vision for Pastors' School, as well as the many ministries and community development projects related to Kafakumba, has had a far-reaching effect in Central Africa.

"I thank my God every time I remember you. In all my prayers for all of you, I always pray with joy because of your partnership in the gospel from the first day."

—Philippians 1:3

Endnote

1. *The Next Christendom: The Coming of Global Christianity,* Philip Jenkins, Oxford University Press, 2002, 198 Madison Avenue, New York, NY 10016

2. Villages are often defined as simply being smaller than towns. In fact, African villages can number in the thousands, even tens of thousands of people at times. What sets them apart is their lack of a municipal center of governance and infrastructure. Villages can feature row upon row of homes, with even small stores or businesses scattered about. But roads, water, and sewage, for example, would not be as developed as they would in a town or city.

Appendix
Letters from the field

Very few of Ken and Lorraine's letters to friends and supporters (generally called Prayer Letters) were saved. Those saved by family members are reprinted here; they give a good sense of the Enright's overall work. A few personal notes were sometimes added for their children and are also included here. Author notes have been added for clarification and are noted in brackets.

Methodist Missionary to Zaire (Congo), Africa, 1978
[Author note: Written and released by Ken and Lorraine when they returned to the United States after the Kolwezi captivity, 1978]

The Reverend and Mrs. Kenneth Enright are coming home from the war torn area of Shaba province in Zaire, where communist guerrillas have been waging war for the last year. They have torn up the church, sacked Mission stations, and executed Dr. Glenn Eschtruth. In spite of the fact that the Enrights were on the Rebel's death list, they stayed and played a key role in reforming the Methodist Mission Program. In May Rev. Enright flew in and rescued his family from the rebels.

When war broke out in the Shaba Province, Mr. Enright piloted a small plane belonging to the Mission. For Mission Personnel in some of the remote areas, the plane was the only means of escape to the cities when fighting neared the stations. During his missionary career, Mr. Enright has served as district superintendent and teacher, as well as evangelist. He has been for the past seven years assigned to the Kolwezi, Kafakumba, and Dilolo Districts where he works with the district Superintendents as a technician in construction of churches.

Born in Chicago, Illinois, Mr. Enright has received degrees from Taylor University and Asbury Seminary. He has done additional study at Northern Baptist Seminary and Kennedy School of Missions at Hartford Theological Seminary. Prior to entering Missionary service he was pastor of churches in Indiana and Ohio.

November 10, 1986
Box 2219
Lubumbashi, Zaire
Dear Friends in Christ:

We have just finished the finest sessions of Pastor's School, and I want to pay tribute to all you who weren't here. Pastors, missionaries, laymen, and praying friends who made this spiritual event possible, and above all this is a tribute to Don and Evelyn MacIntosh who not only have a missionary burden...[Don] also has a number of mission-minded friends. When he got all of us together at Wesley Woods and led us closer to the Holy Spirit, he challenged us and made miracles happen here in Kafakumba.

Speaking about a man from a village, when he chose his name, he probably thought he was being cute. But after a few years of being called "Satan," he became defensive and oppressive. His problems, like his name, became Legion. He was kicked out of school and was in a dead-end rut when he met Kasongo. Kasongo was a young man who loved the Lord and was in our Pastor's school.

He led a local youth choir and "Satan" loved to sing. After he gave his heart to the Lord, the first thing he did was change his name and now wants to become a pastor. Today, he met with Pastor Zacharie, and he is trying to put his marriage back together and go forward in the name of the Lord.

After all these years, it isn't hard to see, "Only Christ can change Africa." And these men are living guideposts showing the way to Christ and transformation.

Lorraine and I consider ourselves blessed in many ways. We are able to see the results of all these years of labor, building this Pastor's School....We want you to be blessed with the knowledge that your ministry is being used by our Lord.

In the little village of Kamafika, this tall man is Supreme....He is the Chief and every little child looks at him as almost a God. They have heard of Mobutu and Reagan, but here he is the living embodiment of all earthly authority. Fear and concern reigned when he became sick and made a long journey to Kafakumba and the Daycare Center dispensary.

His distended stomach indicated a tumor and he needed a flight to the Kapanga Hospital. He was fortunate, as three other emergencies popped up, and I flew with Ken Vance to deliver all these sick folks. It took many hours of flying to cover all the stations, but this old chief stood out in my mind because of the way God literally surrounded him with comfort.

He showed me his large stomach, while Ken Vance was loading the baggage. I teased him that he was pregnant, and his wife just howled with laughter. Just then Mbaka came and gave him 40 Zaires (70 cents) for working in a field, to have money to go to the hospital. When I thought of the pain and work to get 70 cents, I gave him all the money in my pocket...ten dollars, plus a free trip to the hospital. Thus, he had enough. We would provide the medical help free from the dispensary.

As everyone was beginning to get in the plane, he came to me and in all honesty said, Bwana, I'm frightened. This growth, then an airplane, then a hospital in Lunda country. I'm a Christian and so is my wife. Would you pray with us?" I called everyone, and about 50-75 people joined in prayer. It made all the programs that were helping him make sense. Gifts, Wings, Dispensary work, everything, was an expression GOD TAKING CARE OF ONE OF HIS CHILDREN. To the children of Kamafika, he looked big, almost like a God, but in the Arms of the Father, he looked almost like a child.....

As we flew on to Kapanga...I thought....and I decided to write and thank you.

Yours in Christ,
Ken and Lorraine Enright

Lake Kafakumba
January 1987
Dear Friends in Christ,

I always like to get a January letter out to you all, our Friends. Because after the flood of Christmas mail, people like to hear a word of appreciation for all that they and God have done in the year of 1986. For the Enrights, it was a gracious and wonderful blessing to have all our five married children and their families come home to Kafakumba. The friendships, memories, the religious experiences came alive, and to the Africans, this Christmas season has been a living legend.

A number of others came to spend Christmas with us and there were twenty-three of us that sat down together. Most of the year we are here alone, and this was quite a contrast. Especially to have little Grandchildren running around opening presents, and keeping everybody busy. Now with Lena Eschtruth living with us, she and Lorraine share the work and it makes it much nicer.

The Day Care Center is now working out of Kafakumba and has saved many people's lives. Lena has been carrying on an immunization program and Lorraine has a steady stream of malnourished children at the back door every day.

We had a large Evangelistic celebration and invited every new Christian to come and give their testimony. The older Christians came also, and we had over a thousand people all together. About 200 seekers came to the altar and another hundred witnessed to a new experience in Christ. We ate three sheep, two pigs, and a goat. We distributed hundreds of gospels of John and Home Study Courses, which the Pastors will follow up in April. Every needy person was given clothes and help, thanks to Fowler supporters, Day Care supporters, and others who make our work possible.

I will enclose a number of slip sheets which will give you a better picture of our work. However, we want this letter to express our personal heartfelt thanks to God for bringing your prayers and support into our ministry.

Your friends in Christ,
Kenneth and Lorraine Enright

[Author note: This was a personal note attached to son, Ken, and his wife Denise]

Guess what? I just ran out of bananas. Imagine—here at Kafakumba! A lady brought me green ones this morning. [Author's note: Bananas were raised at Kafakumba in order to feed the many children who came to the Enright back door each morning. Lorraine often said that she "would never run out of bananas" in relation to the feeding program, but sometimes she evidently did.]

Lena (Eschtruth) leaves in March for furlough. We all go to Luena soon and then on the Boat (the *Kipindano*) to Mulongo, doing Evangelistic work, Bible distribution, and T.B. vaccination on the way. We plan to leave here the last of May and take a little time on the way home. We need your prayers.

Lots of Love,
Mom and Dad

Easter 1988
Dear Friends in Christ,

We have been back a month and it is time I write and share how the work is going. The trip out was lovely and we got a big shipment of medicines in London, which came through without any hassle. All our old friends look good, but they have aged so much I am afraid to look in the mirror. Rainy season is at its zenith, and the roads are impassable, but the young Pilots have taken us everywhere, so that we could pick up the threads of our programs and see our children. My how these young pilots serve the church in a wonderful way. WINGS OF THE MORNING IS SUPPLYING THE LIFELINE TO EVERYONE…THE SICK…THE EVANGELISTIC PROGRAMS… THE BISHOP AND ADMINISTRATION, AS WELL AS MISSIONARY FAMILIES.

I am preaching an Easter Revival, and yesterday we had a new type of service, where the Christians confessed their sins and stood and declared their faith in Christ. Then, we consecrated ourselves to love and serve Him. More than two hundred went through this act of faith. An old man stopped by as he began his walk back to his village and said, "I am different, God has done something. And I am going home to a new life." Truly the proofs of Easter aren't empty tombs and repeated stories, but filled hearts and changed lives. We are glad to be back home this EASTER.

I am also a realist and don't want to portray only the lovely...I have a truck stuck in the mud axel deep with a transmission bearing shot and a universal joint torn out. It is near Mutshatsha and about two hundred miles from here. I am hoping to get it running this week in time to pick up the pastors and begin hauling them here. Our main generator was damaged while I was gone and I shipped it to the city to get a Mining engineer to fix it. If a number of you hadn't given offerings and gifts direct, I would be absolutely blocked, and so I want to thank you, and say it is only nice being here because you enable us to meet these needs.

Thanks again for making God's work possible here in Zaire.

Your friends in Christ,
Ken and Lorraine Enright

June 18, 1988
Lake Kafakumba
Dear Elinda and Nate:

As you can see I am having fun and the work is going along just fine. We wonder about the Steury's and their trip back to the field. We also wonder how you all are doing now that you're out of school. I understand John, Ken and crowd are all in Hillman [Author note: Lorraine's hometown in Michigan] and are fishing. I hope they get out for salmon as Nate and I did.

Mother and Lena have certainly changed everything here and the Dispensary and Daycare Center are really progressing. It kills me to look at the little kids each morning that line up for food. SO I JUST DON'T LOOK AT THEM. I hire all the women and pay them to work for a half day on the airstrip or at the garden. Thus, they can eat and pay for their treatment. So write when you can and we send all our love.

Dear Ken and Denise:

Father's Day is this Sunday so I'm watching the mail. The three Wolford families were here, Ken Vance and Debbie, and Lowell and Claudia, and Dan and Crystal were here for about a week so it's been a real social season, as well as a great Pastor's School. I heard about the drought, and I want to invite you all down to share my bumper crop. My dry season garden is a real success so I'm going to put in permanent irrigation and have a dry season crop each year.

Paul Harvey just whets my appetite to know what's going on. How about mailing me a couple copies of Fortune to the Kitwe Box? I'd love them. Plus the first two pages of a couple of Wall Street Journals.

From Lake Kafakumba
Dear John, Kendy, and Boys,

I promised mother if I shot 45 on nine holes I would write you this letter tonight. [Author note: Ken was just finishing the construction of a small nine-hole golf course at Lake Kafakumba at this time.] We just finished a fish filet supper and mother and Lena are patching a chair and packing as Lena will return tomorrow to Luena. [Author note: Lena Eschtruth was the widow of Dr. Glen Eschtruth, killed by rebels at Kapanga Hospital. She was a nurse and spent a lot of time at Lake Kafakumba and with the Enrights, helping with their Dispensary and taking vaccination out into local villages. Luena was another Methodist mission station about an hour from Kafakumba.] We are going to stay here another week or ten days as I want to get the building up for the Laboratory. I've gone all-hog and am building a 22 x

7 meter building with two wards as well as a Depot and Laboratory.

We've really poured money into the station and it really is getting into nice shape. Down along the water near the edge of the airstrip we have a big dry-season garden. Lowell has the beacon working and also put up my antenna for Amateur (radio). We should be getting through to you folks soon. The golf course is really coming and I would like five or ten pounds of good grass seed for the greens.

Pastor's School was a real wonderful experience and we are looking forward to August. We hope to spend two weeks dividing the school according to Conferences and spend them at Sandoa and Kanene. We want Ntambo [Author note: Ntambo Nkulu went on to become the bishop of North Katanga Conference in Congo] to head up the Kanene School with all the new men and concentrate on village evangelism. Zombil and Zackary will head up Sandoa and we will visit both places. Then they will come here for the remaining period. We will also pass out Bibles and run Bible classes.

I bought 20 bags of corn and have another forty to pick up. So when Nawej comes back from the city I will send a load of corn over to Luena to grind. This gives me back loads on the trucks. I am running about 90 sheep. We lost one today because a smart African conned me into buying one that was blind. She literally couldn't find food or water and starved before I found out. We killed a few young males that you castrated. They were big and reached their full growth. We have four from Mitwaba that you bought. They are all with young, and we hope they'll give birth soon. Dan couldn't believe the number of twins we're getting. Incidentally, we have another load of pineapple plants from Kapanga, 25 citrus trees, sugar cane by the lake, and rice that is almost a foot tall in the edge of the swamp. Beans and tomatoes are enough for the dispensary so you see my work is going on.

Your friends in Christ,
Ken and Lorraine Enright

March 20, 1989
[Author note: Written from Florida, just before returning to Congo.]
Dear Friends in Christ,

We're done! Our last preaching service is finished. It is time to quit preaching and start packing. We leave in three weeks, and I know in my heart that between now and the time we get on the plane, there will be more tiredness, frustration, and pain.

However, there is a bright spot in the garage. One huge pile is medicines that will be saving thousands of lives. It represents your gifts to the Day Care Center. Laboratory equipment worth thousands of dollars has been donated to help us see the medicals problems we have to solve.

Two hundred and fifty fruit trees are being packed, irrigation equipment, seeds from Ohio, and a spiritual banner. All of these things are on the way to help make Christ known. As I stop and wipe the sweat from my weary brow, I can't help but rejoice and think of you! There is enough money to pay for the freight. One church sent a check and paid for Lorrain's and my tickets to return to Zaire. We're looking forward to a number of ministries—Wings of the Morning Flight Ministry, Kafakumba Pastors' School, and the Lorraine Enright Day Care Center. We are prayerfully hoping to come back to the States in October and tell churches what we did with their gifts. A number of churches have already started to book us for services. I want you to know this for two reasons: If you have some tithe or a gift you want us to take with us, please send it to the address below. If you want us to come and share with your church, write us at the address below. We know we can't take all the speaking engagements as some are already committed.

We have received a number of messages from Zaire. The chauffeur, Mawej, said, "Come, I need help fixing this truck." Roj, our nurse, begged us to hurry back. He is treating over one hundred a day at the Dispensary. Lena Eschtruth has worked in these programs and carried the weight long enough and wants us back. But Mosh's widow wants us just to share Jesus. She is lonely and her husband is gone.

We're standing in the garage packing suitcases. Our minds are all over the U.S. with you, but our hearts have already left and are on their way home to Africa.

Please….PRAY, WRITE, AND GIVE so that on our return God allows us to celebrate a successful ministry together…Celebrating Christ in all and for all.

Love and prayers,
Ken and Lorraine
921 Sandcrest Dr
Port Orange, FL 32019

May 26, 1989
Kafakumba, Zaire
Dear Friends in Christ:

Today is our 44th Anniversary and I have been sitting here remembering all the blessings God has bestowed on our marriage, family, and ministry here in Africa. When God made us one and blessed that oneness by becoming one with us, Life has been just plain wonderful…even during the bad patches. My advice to our Pastors is, "MARRIAGE IS WONDERFUL BUT FRAGILE…DON'T TAKE ANYTHING OR ANYONE FOR GRANTED." An old vow or a forgotten gift can't replace a hug and kiss today.

Here at Kafakumba amongst the pastor school students, many suffer from broken marriages and Africa hurts from this plague. The TV evangelists, the modern American lifestyle, and the scandals show how fragile love is. I just heard of one couple of 47 years who broke up. I know twelve missionary couples that have lost out. Most took too much for granted and ended with too little too late.

Fortifying Christian marriages, we stress allowing God's Holy Spirit to control all phases of our faith, family, and ministry.

Taking nothing for granted we try to tell our loved ones how important they are in our walk with God. THIS SCHOOL MINISTERS TO THE WIVES AND CHILDREN ALSO.

THERE IS A STRONG PARRALEL HERE IN MISSIONS. We appreciate the way you have joined us in making Christ known here in Zaire. The gifts of money, food, medicines, and prayer are never taken for granted. I know a financial crisis, a change of pastor, a lost letter, attacks the fragility of Missions. YET I MARVEL HOW GOD HAS CONTINUED TO BLESS THE ONENESS THAT SUPPORTS THIS MINISTRY. We want you to know we love the fact that YOU are a part of our lives and ministry. Please continue to prayerfully support KAFAKUMBA PASTORS' SCHOOL, THE DAY CARE CENTER, AND WINGS FLIGHT MINISTRY.

ONE HUNDREND PASTORS RECEIVED NEW BIKES...THAT'S $20,000.

TODAY THESE PASTORS LEFT AND ARE HOLDING WEEKEND MEETINGS COVERING 2,500 SQUARE MILES. Don't take it for granted; we're praying for them.

While we were home they treated an average of 22 starving babies a day, saving hundreds of lives...Your gifts lift a song of praise to Jesus. Daycare is eternal.

Exuberance over success isn't enough, don't take anything for granted.

Your friends in Christ,
Ken and Lorraine Enright

June 1989
[Author note: This is an excerpt from a letter that also included this note from the wife of the Bishop of Southern Congo, Mama Bishop Katembo, Lubumbashi.]
Dear Baba and Mama Enright,

My joy came from the fact that the teachings were from the heart and I have been praising and thanking God that he sent you here to Africa preaching and sharing Christ. You have been used of God to give sight to the blind, open our deaf ears, and heal the cripple and sick, and the poor are being healed in Soul as well as body. You are bringing us to Christ. These are the first teachings I ever received on the Holy Spirit, and I want to share all of this with our preachers and their wives in our conference.

Thanks for coming, and I pray you will prayerfully keep on. You helped me by the way you taught with strength and happiness.

Ken: YOUR SUPPORT AND HELP MADE THIS HAPPEN!!! The thanks is to you.

[Author note: A letter notifying supporters of Ken and Lorraine's retirement.]

What about the Enrights?
Are they retired or not?
No!!! We have gone "off-salary" but we still have our Conference Appointments as Directors of the Kafakumba Pastors' School and the Day Care Centers. We will spend six months of each year on the field and then return to raise development funds for Methodist work.

Do they still need our support or not?
This fight has gone on for over forty years....There are some in New York that hate funds going straight to the field and not taking the scenic route through 475 Riverside Drive so

everyone can get credit and a piece of the action. One church did a nice thing…they took our Salary support and bought our tickets to return in three weeks. Support sent direct will be there in three weeks instead of eighteen months. [Author note: Ken was encouraging supporters to send funds through the nonprofit organization that had been organized to support their work in Congo. Before technology enabled quicker and more transparent handling of monies, gifts given through local churches sometimes took months to travel through the system.]

Are they still available for speaking?

We will be speaking next fall and winter. BUT WRITE US NOW AS DATES ARE FILLING UP, AND I DON'T WANT TO TAKE NEW ENGAGEMENTS AND NEGLECT YOU FOLKS WHO HAVE SUPPORTED US THROUGH THE YEARS.

How is their health?

Our doctor just gave us a WONDERFUL REPORT, AND WE ARE FINE. Ever since I went to the altar at Cherry Run my eyes have slowed down the deterioration and are holding up fairly good. PRAISE THE LORD.

A letter to supporters at the time of Ken's death:

Rev. Kenneth D. Enright
July 27, 1922-June 9, 2006
June 25, 2006 –The Rev. Kenneth Enright, who gave his life in missionary service in the Congo, died in Zambia on June 9 at the age of 83.

Kenneth Enright was a native of Chicago, born there July 27th, 1922, where he grew up through his high school years. He graduated from Taylor University in Indiana in 1945 and from Asbury Theological Seminary in Kentucky in 1948. He also studied at Northern Baptist Theological Seminary and earned his Master's Degree in missions from Kennedy School of Missions in Hartford, Connecticut. He held several student pastorates while in school, and was a deacon when he entered missionary service. He went on to become a clergy member of the South Congo Annual Conference of the United Methodist Church where he spent most of his career.

Yet despite all his professional training, Ken was first and foremost a pastor who loved leading others to Christ. His gift of evangelism earned him the nickname, "the Billy Graham of Africa."

Ken and his wife both felt a strong calling to ministry in Africa at early ages. They were married in 1945 and had five children: Kenneth, John, Elaine, Eileen, and Elinda. Both Elaine and John would also become missionaries, and all their children continue to be involved in some aspect of mission support.

He and his wife, Lorraine, served as missionaries from 1948 until 1998, in what is today the Democratic Republic of Congo. At the time of his death, he was in Zambia serving with his son and daughter-in-law, the Rev. John and Kendra Enright.

"Ken Enright was a legendary mission figure in Congo," said the Rev. R. Randy Day, chief executive of the General Board of Global Ministries, the international mission agency of the United Methodist Church. "He and his wife may have *formally* retired along the way, but both retained the missionary calling. Ken was in mission to the very end."

Bibliography and Related Resources

Amstutz, Harold W.
Beyond the Monkey Paw: A Missionary Pilot's Story
Word Association Publishers
205 Fifth Ave
Tarentum, PA
2001

Britannica Online Encyclopedia
www.britannica.com
December 2012

Dawson, David M.D.
No Fear in His Presence
Regal Books
1957 Eastman Avenue
Ventura CA 93003
1980

Hartzler, Eva Coates
Brief History of Methodist Missionary work in the Southern Congo
  During the First Fifty Years
The Methodist Church of Southern Congo
Elizabethville (now Lubumbashi)
1960

Jenkins, Philip
The Next Christendom: The Coming of Global Christianity
Oxford University Press
198 Madison Avenue
New York, NY 10016
2002

Jenkins, Philip
*The New Faces of Christianity: Believing the Bible in the Global
     South*
Oxford University Press
198 Madison Avenue
New York, NY 10016
2006

Munza, Kasongo
A Letter to Africa about Africa
Kafakumba Training Center
Google books
2005

Shell, Virginia Law
Appointment Congo
P. O. Box 98764
Raleigh, NC 27624

Springer, John M.
Pioneering in the Congo, Second Edition
The Katanga Press
150 Fifth Avenue
New York, NY
Printed by The Methodist Book Concern (now United
     Methodist Publishing)
1917

Time magazine
June 11, 1978
"Inside Kolwezi: Toll of Terror, Rebels are gone, but fear lingers
    on."

CPSIA information can be obtained
at www.ICGtesting.com
Printed in the USA
FSOW04n1155201016
26371FS

9 781457 520624